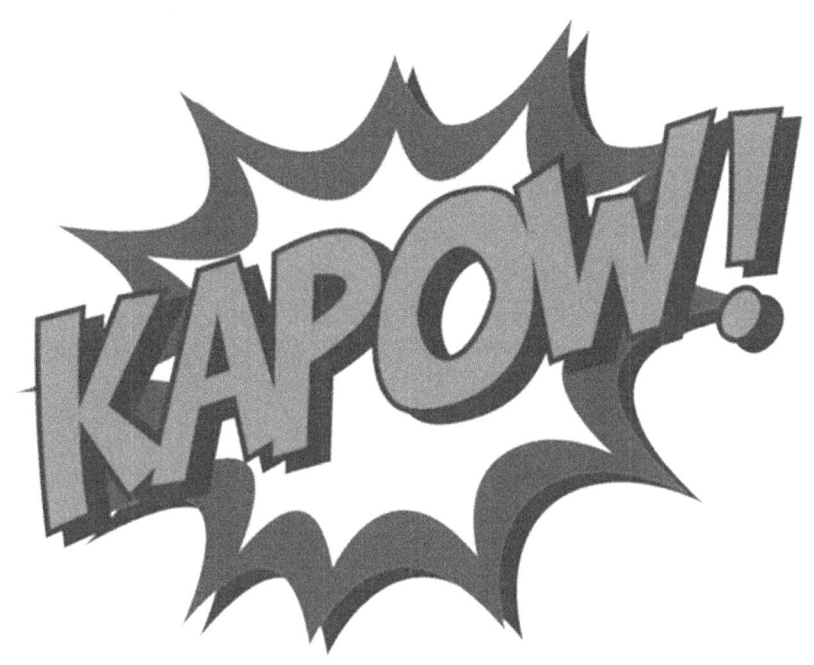

The Ultimate Pop Art Coloring Book!!

By Mary Sol

Completely done with coloring boring mandalas and flowers?

Well look no further because KAPOW!! The Ultimate Pop Art Coloring Book is here to help you relax and spend time doing your favorite activity with fun awesome illustrations.
Within this coloring book, you will be able to find comic-style drawings, retro and old school illustrations, fun psychedelic images and pop art inspired mosaics.
The only rule? Use as many colors as you want! The Brighter the better!

Mar y Sol

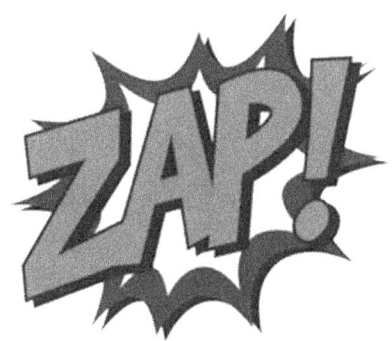

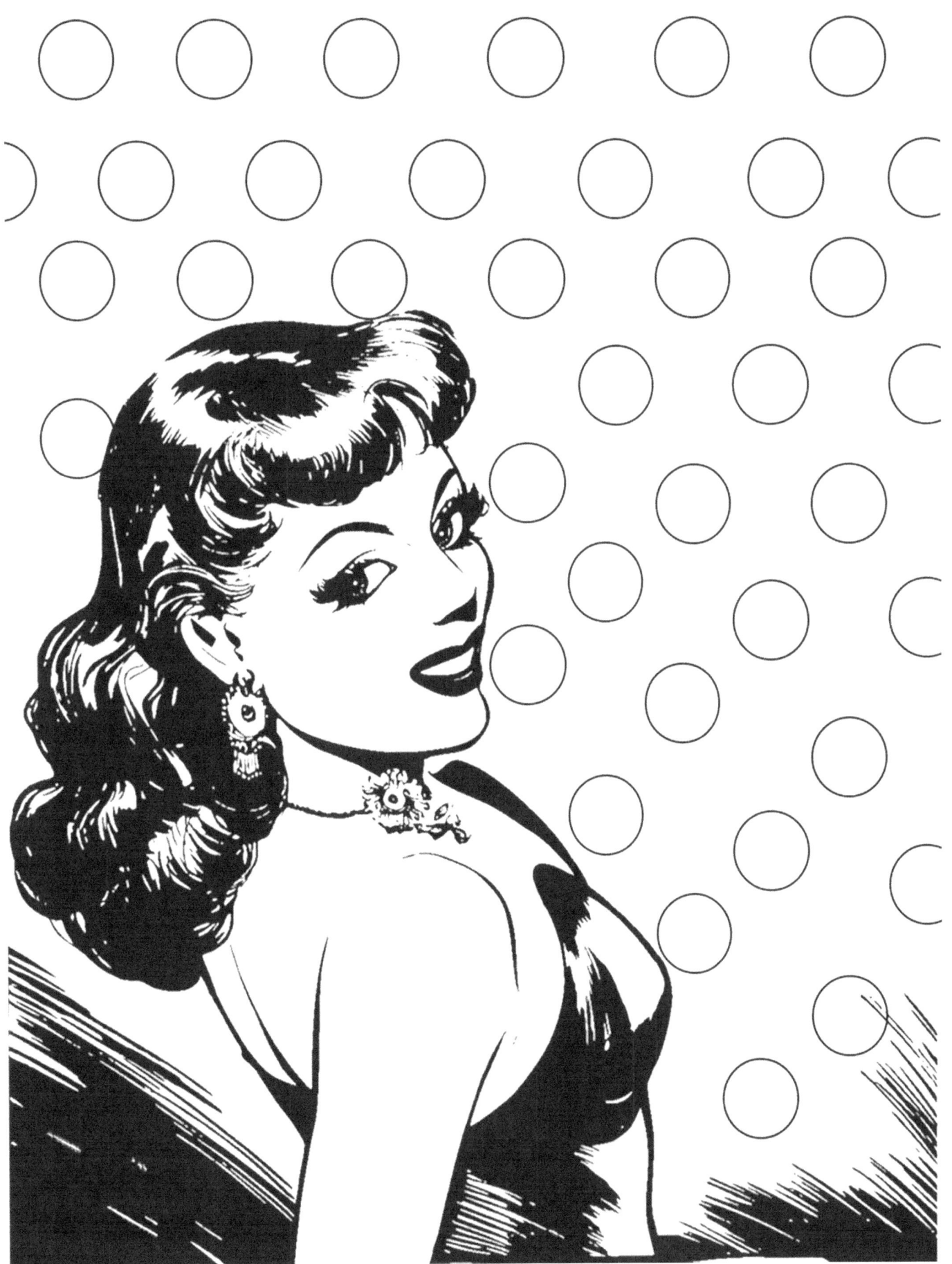

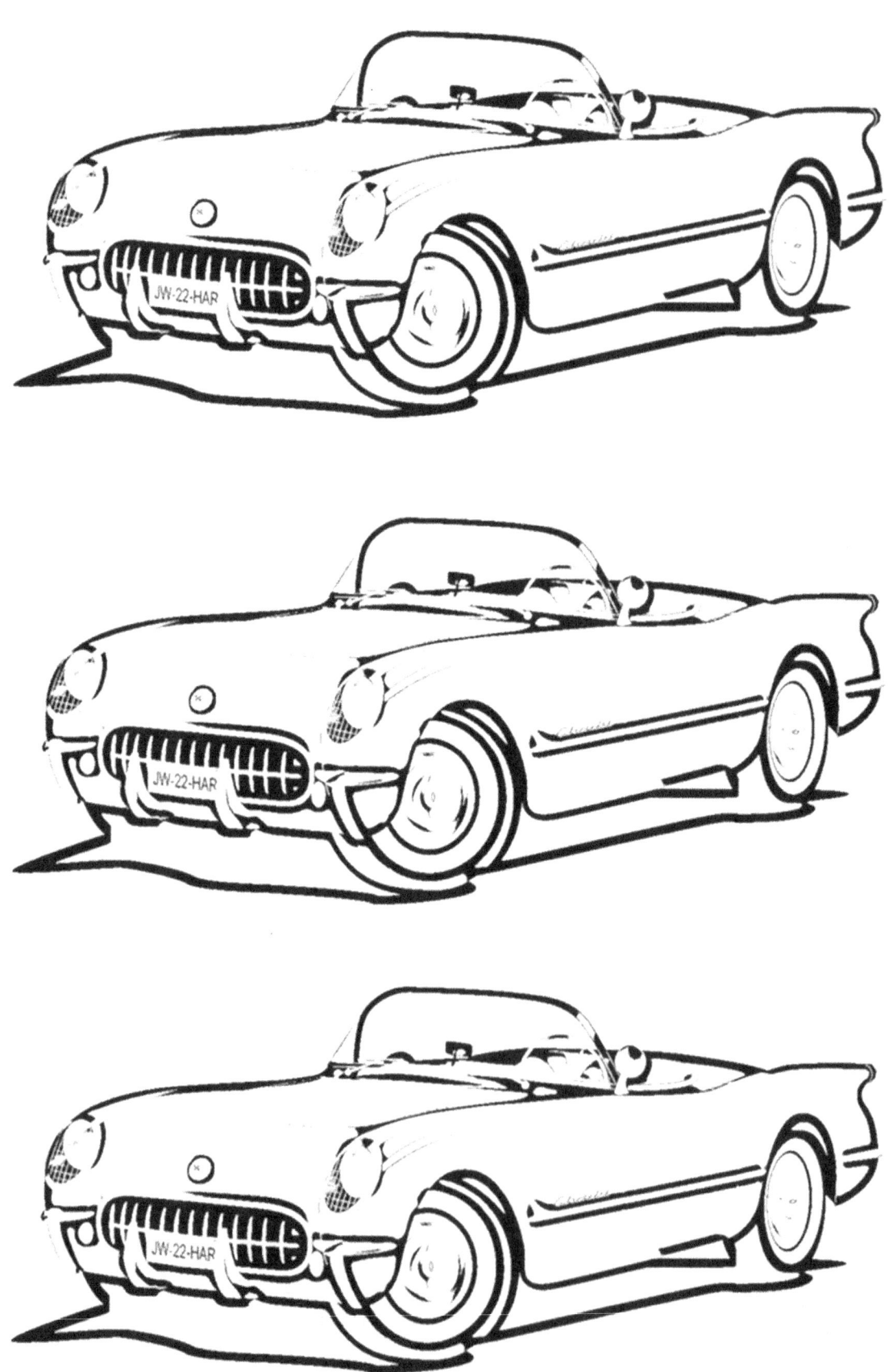

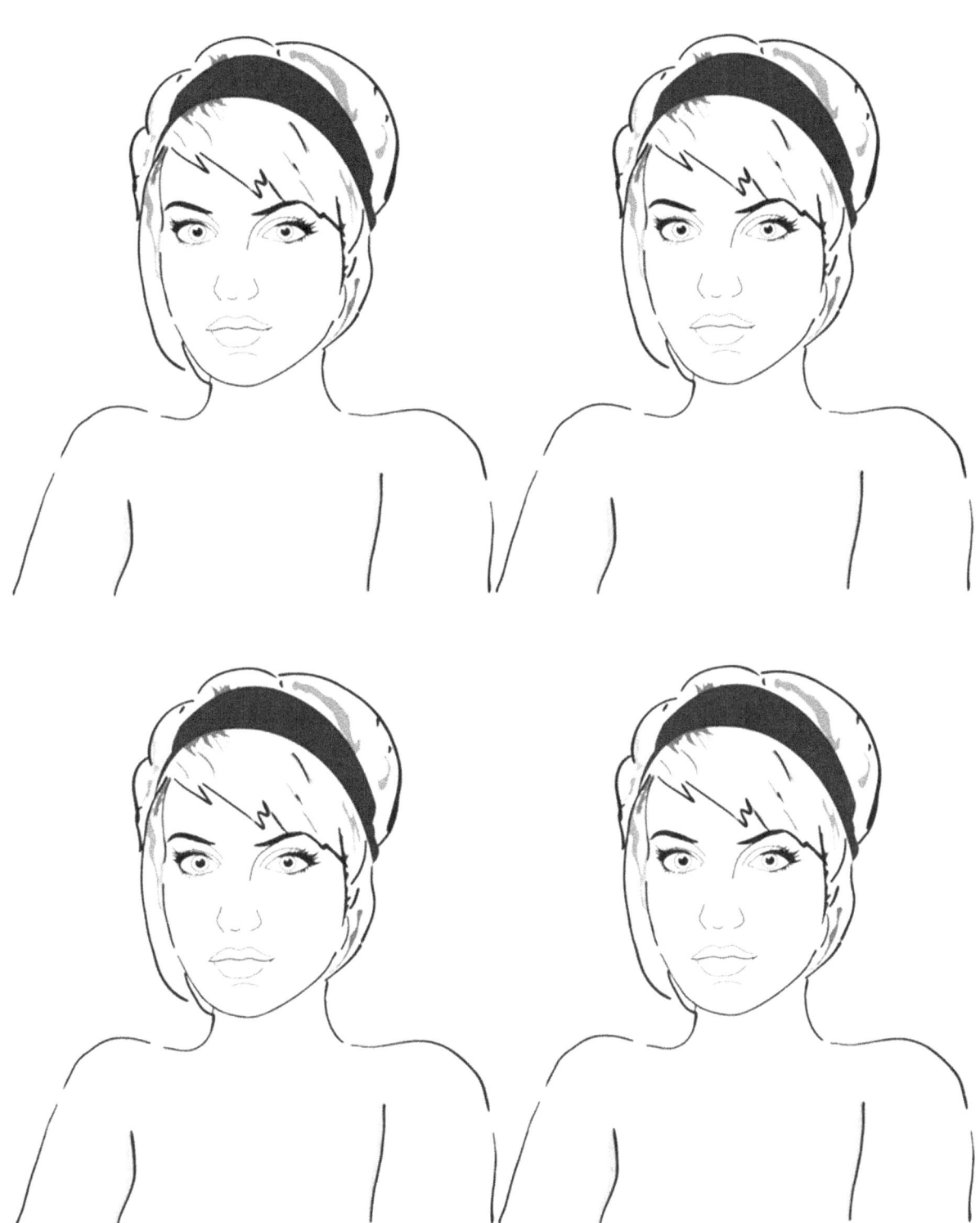

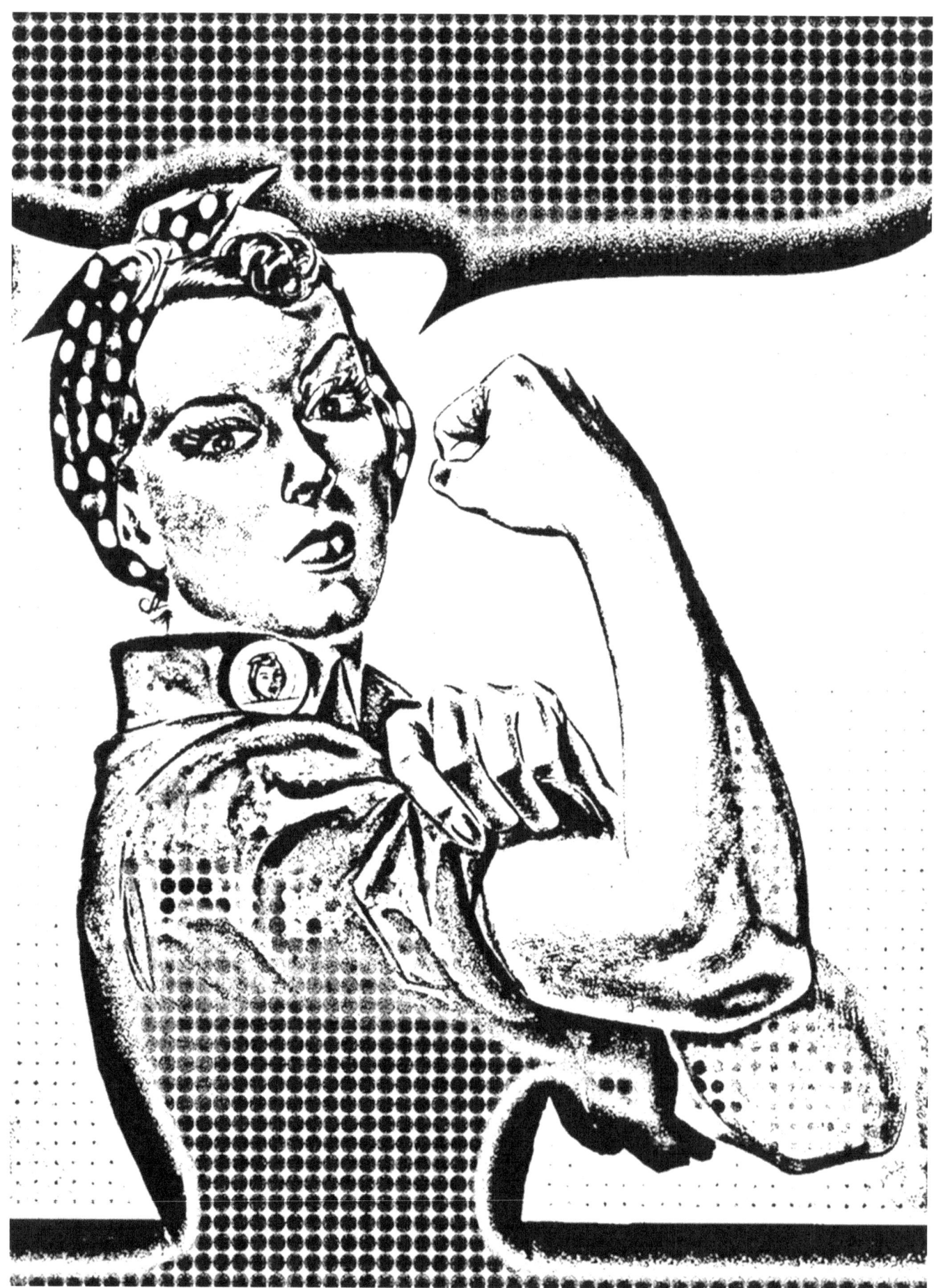

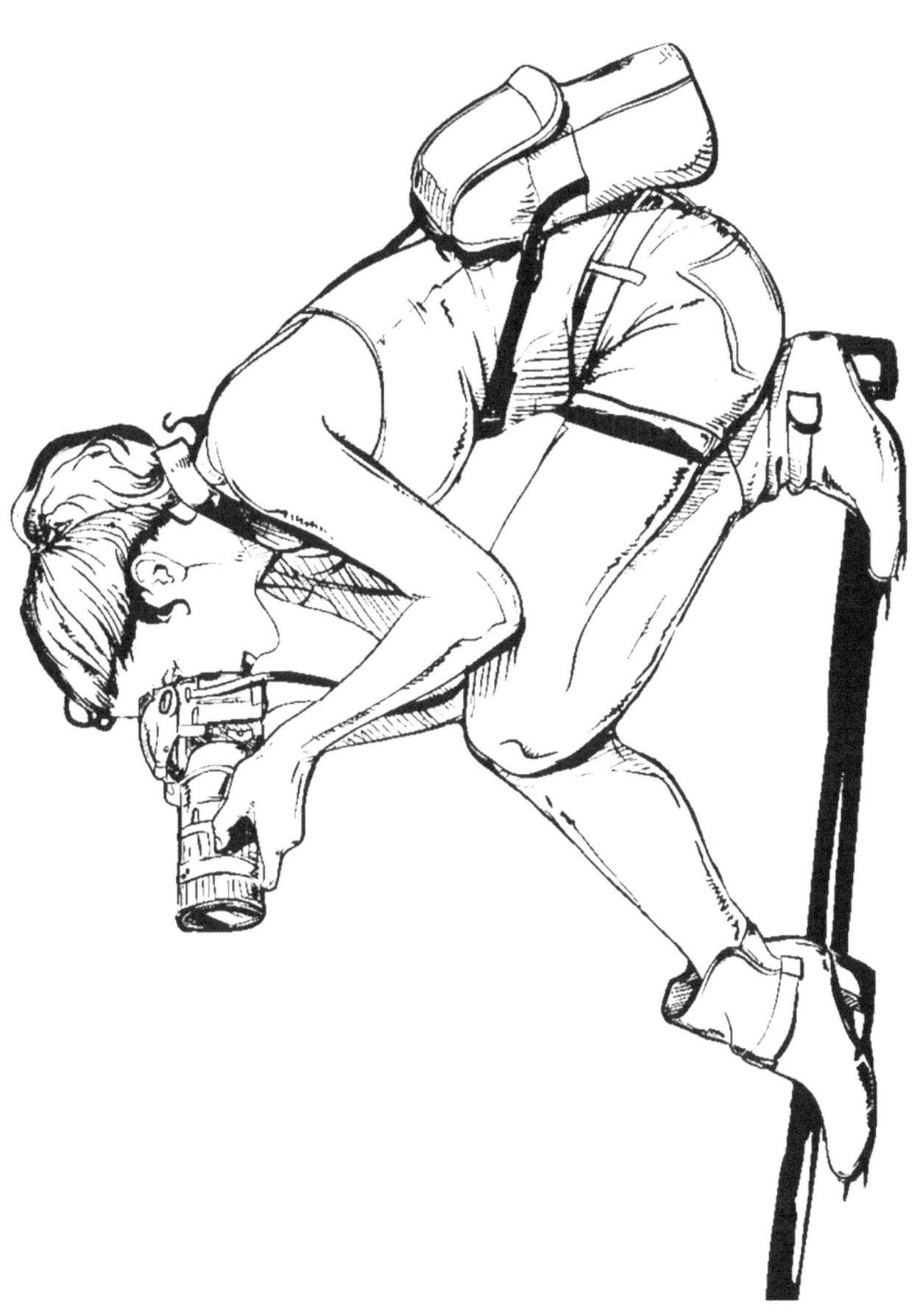

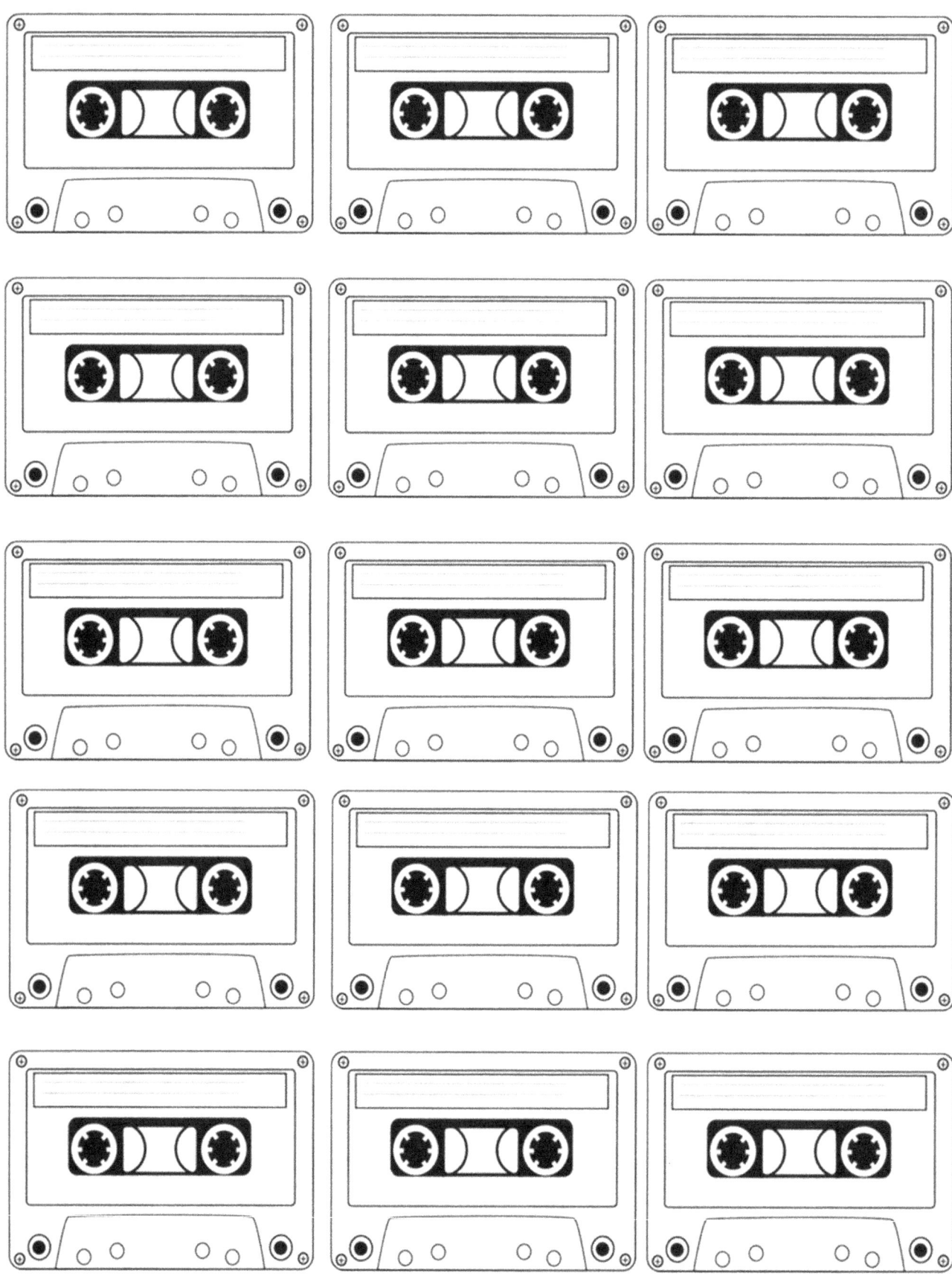

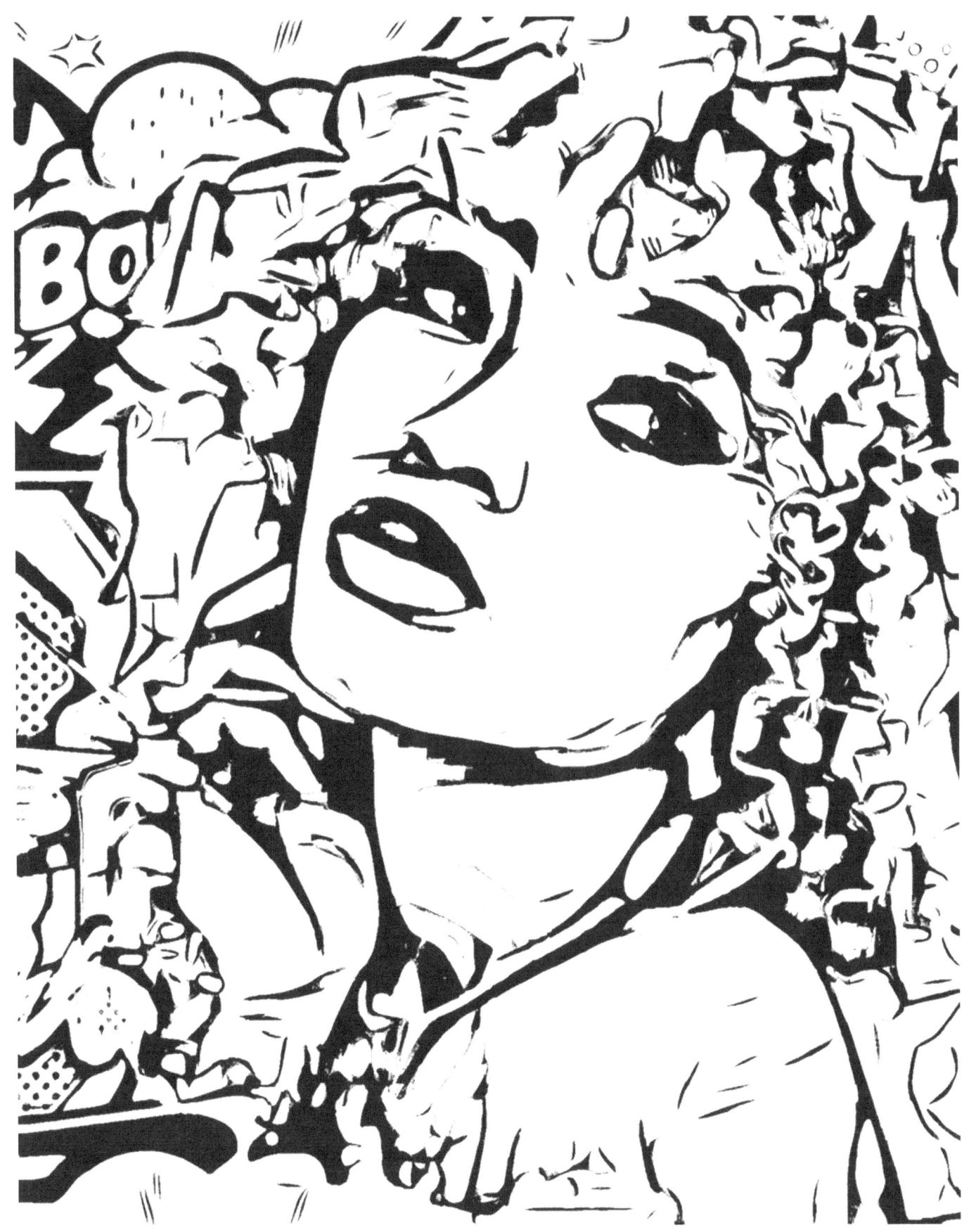

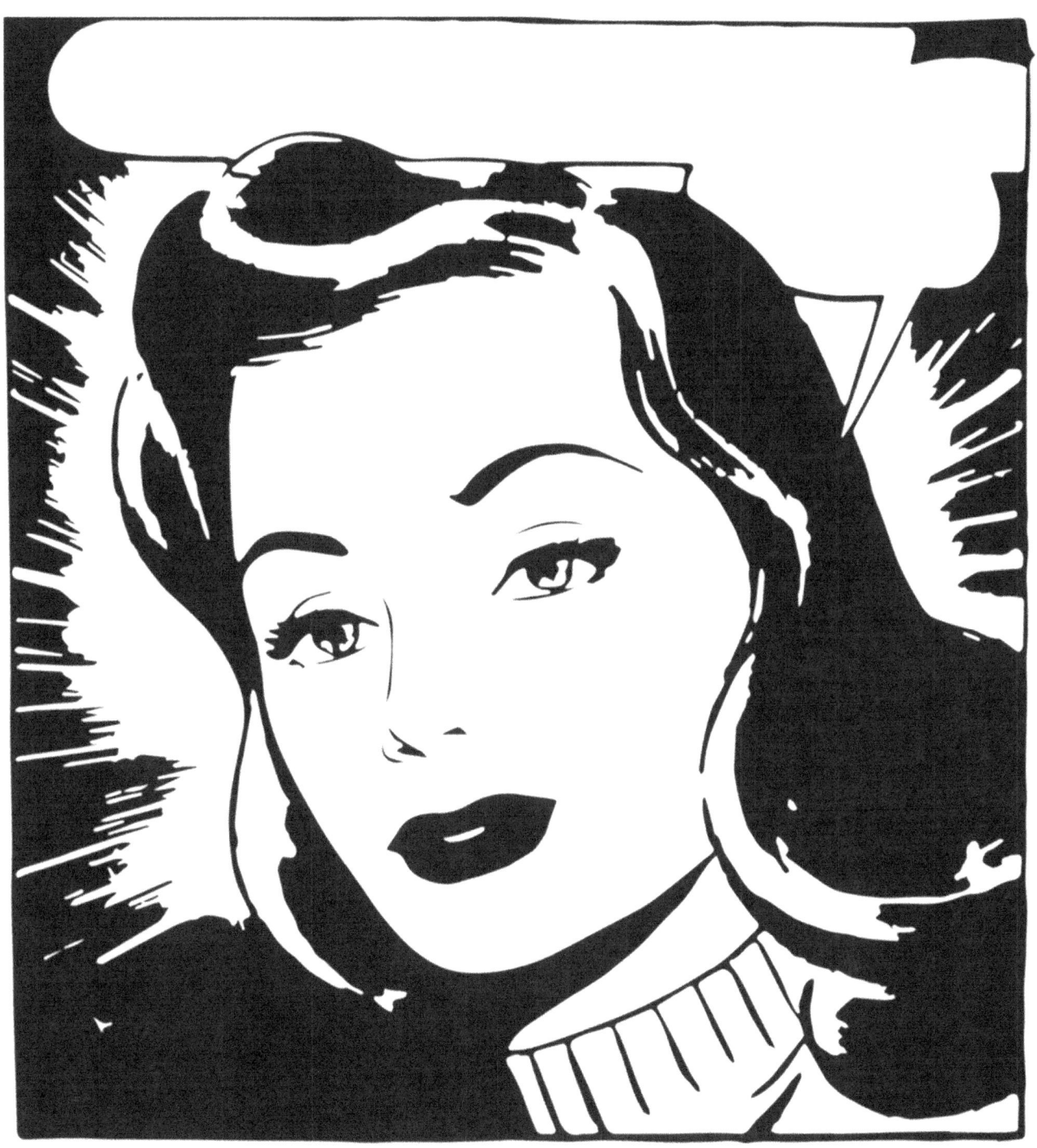

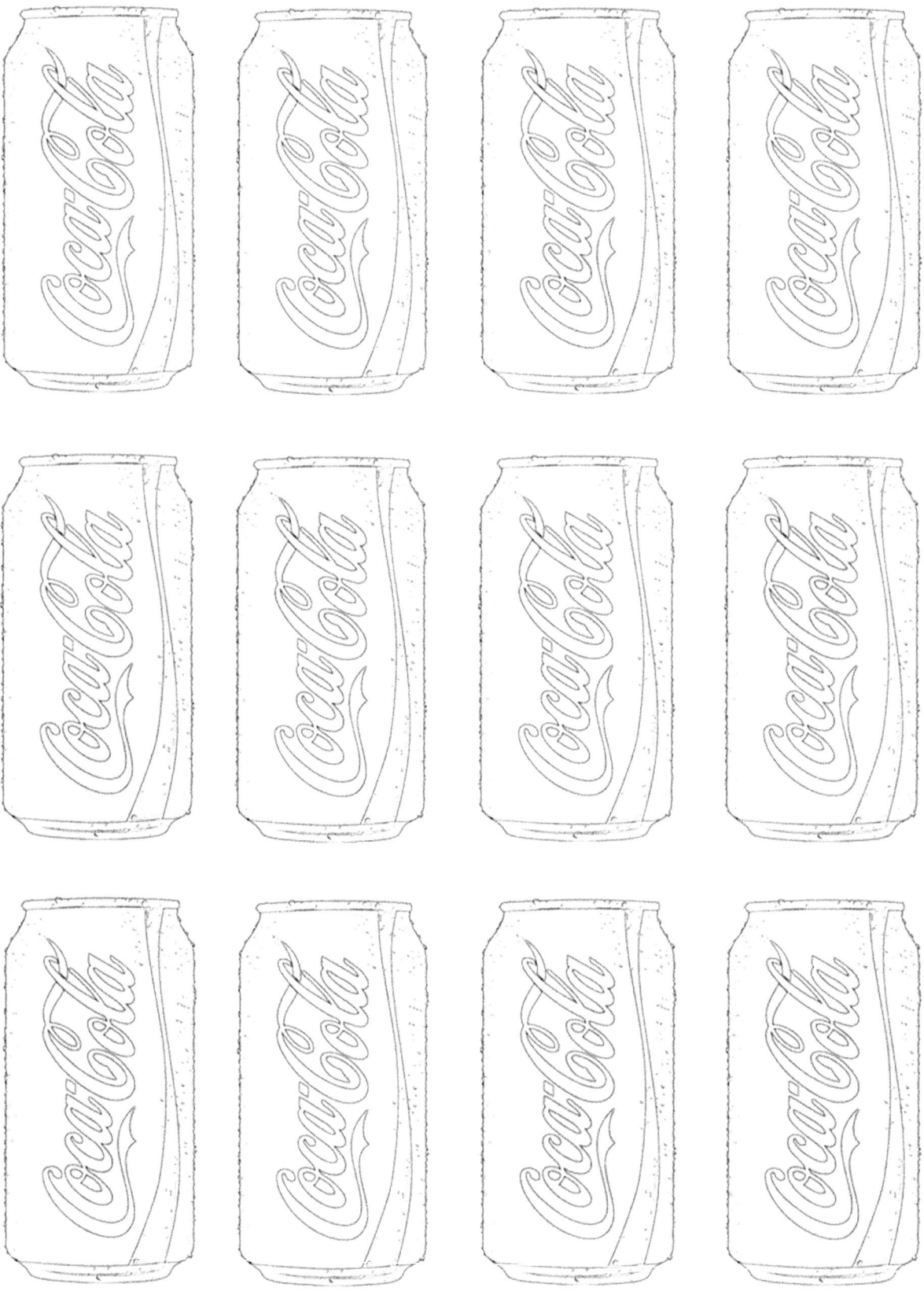

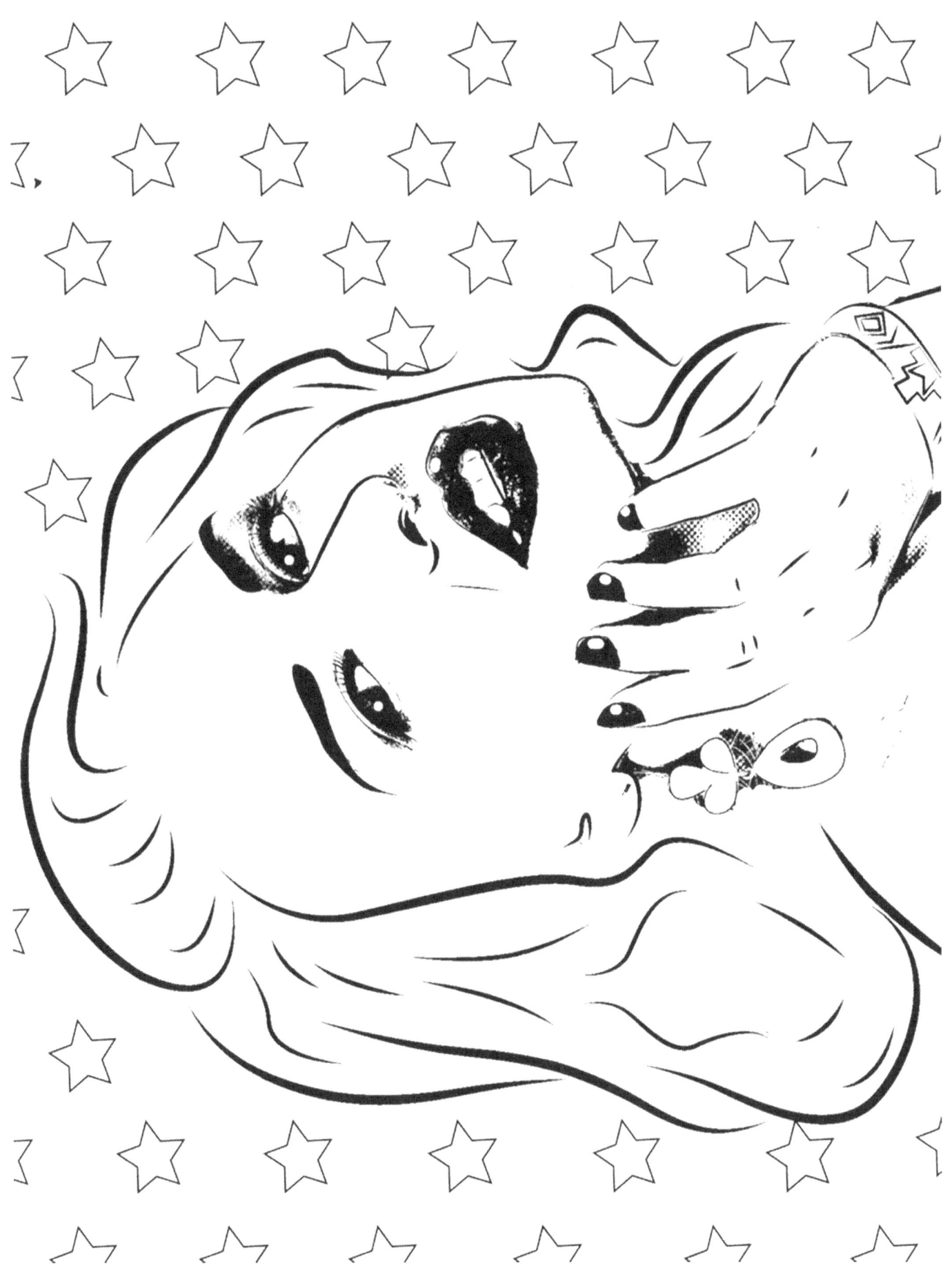

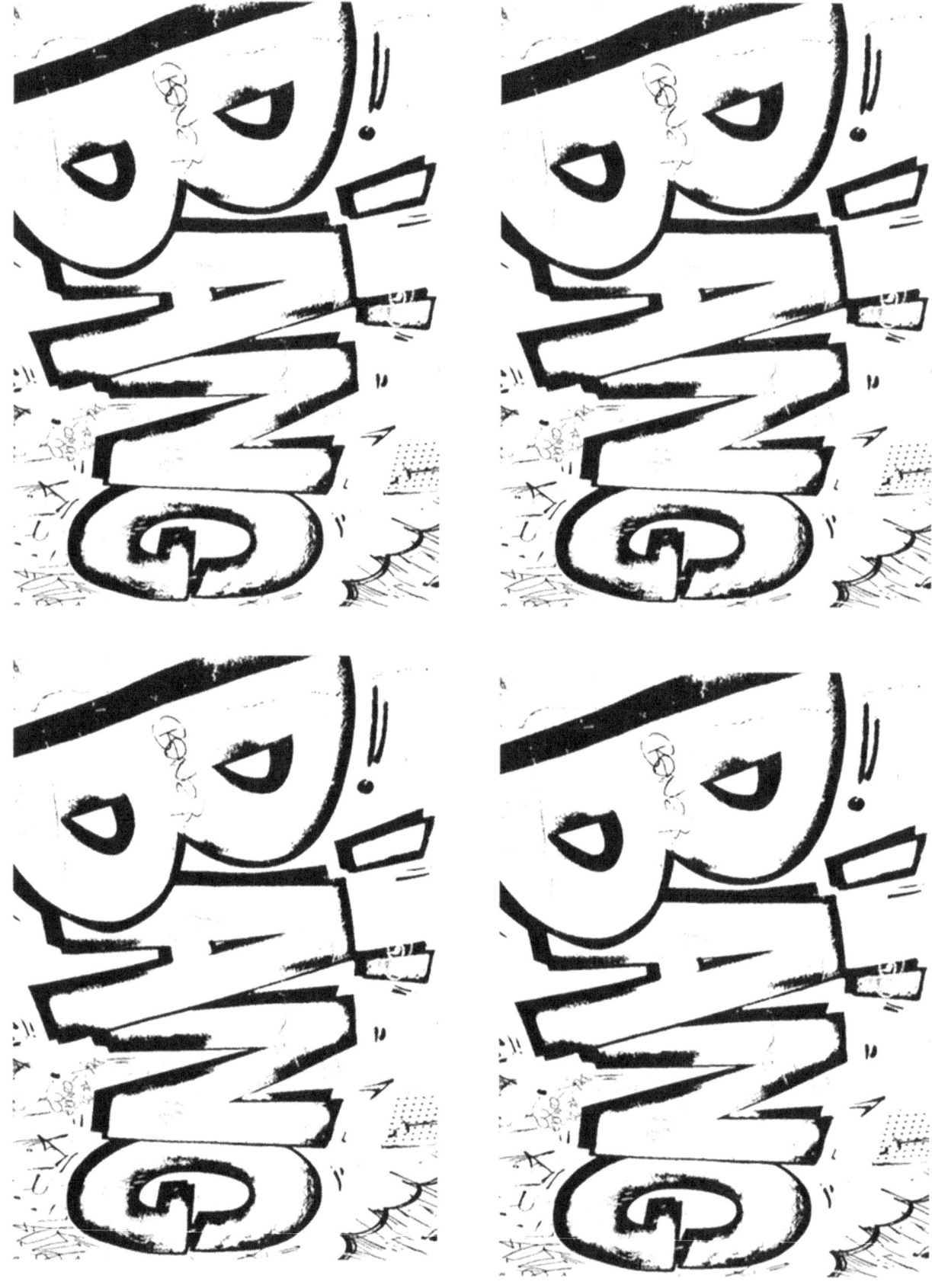

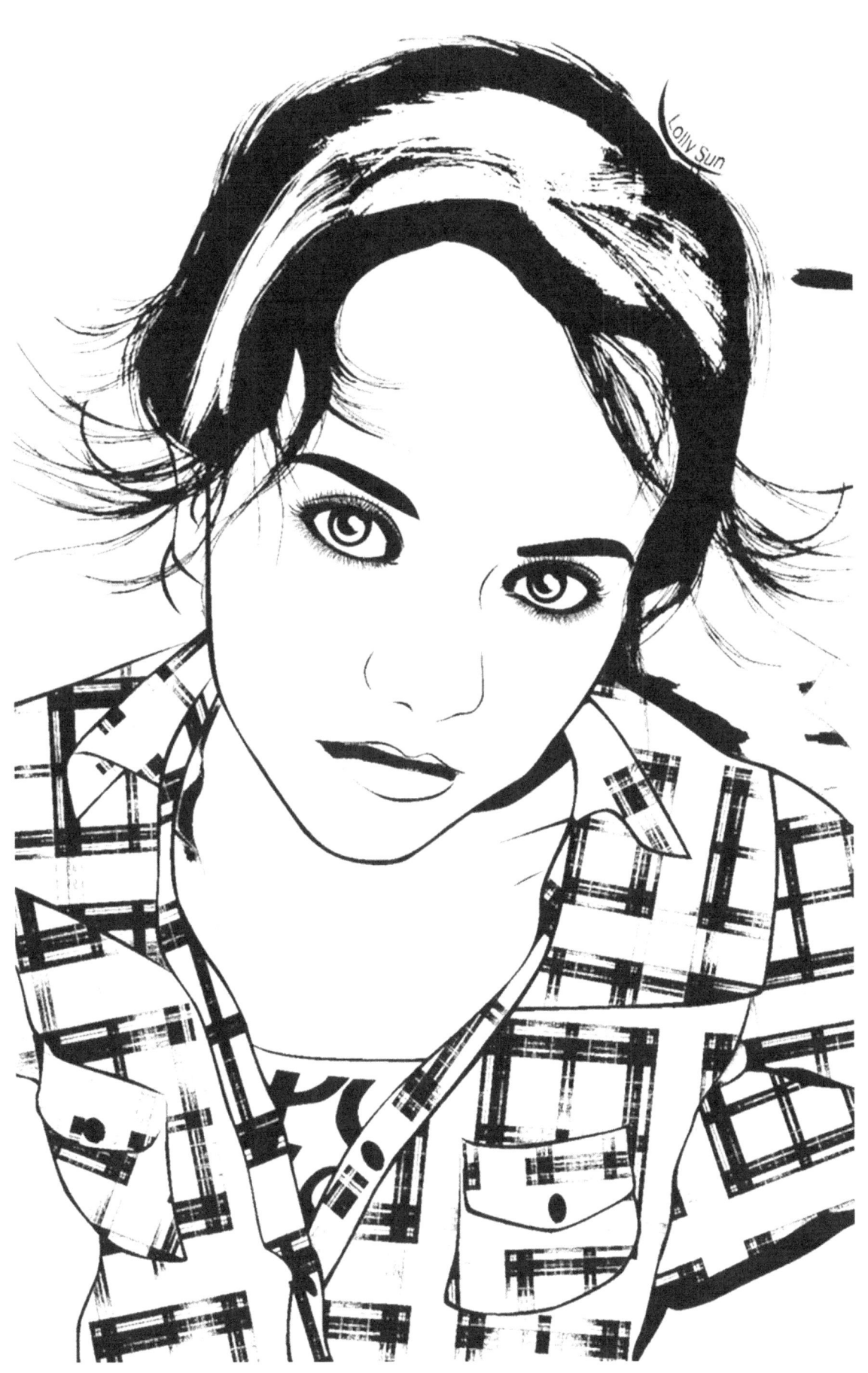

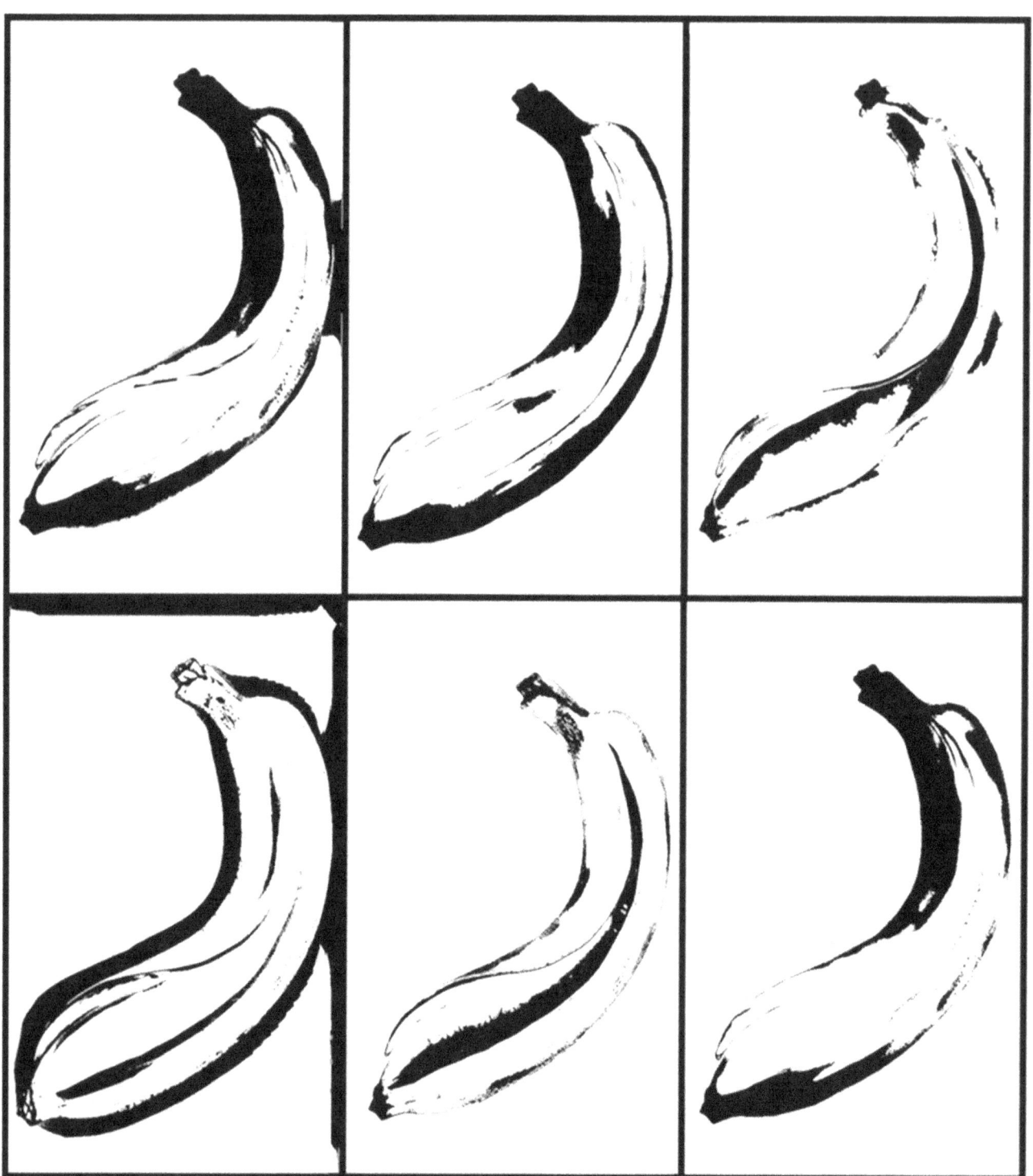

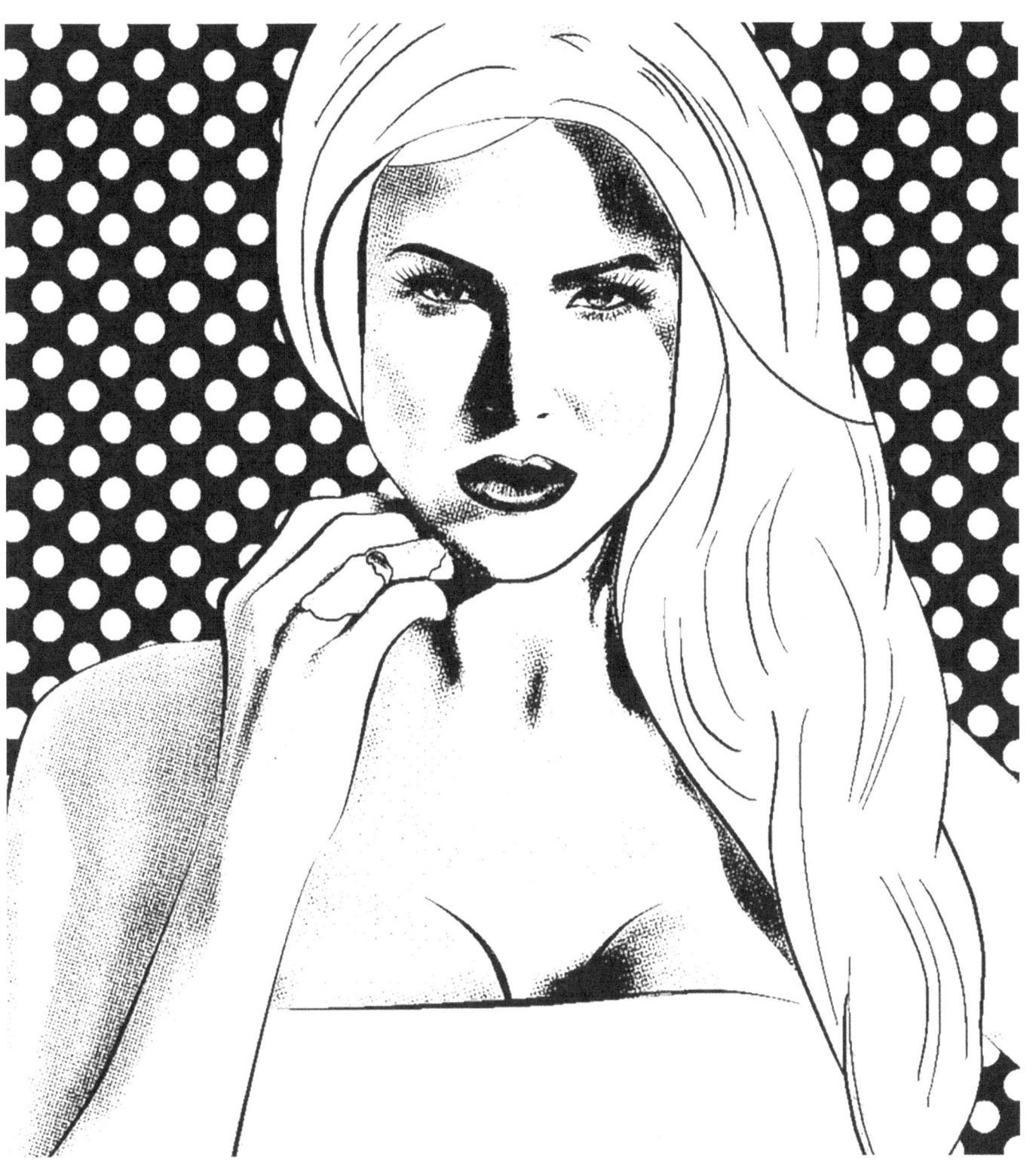

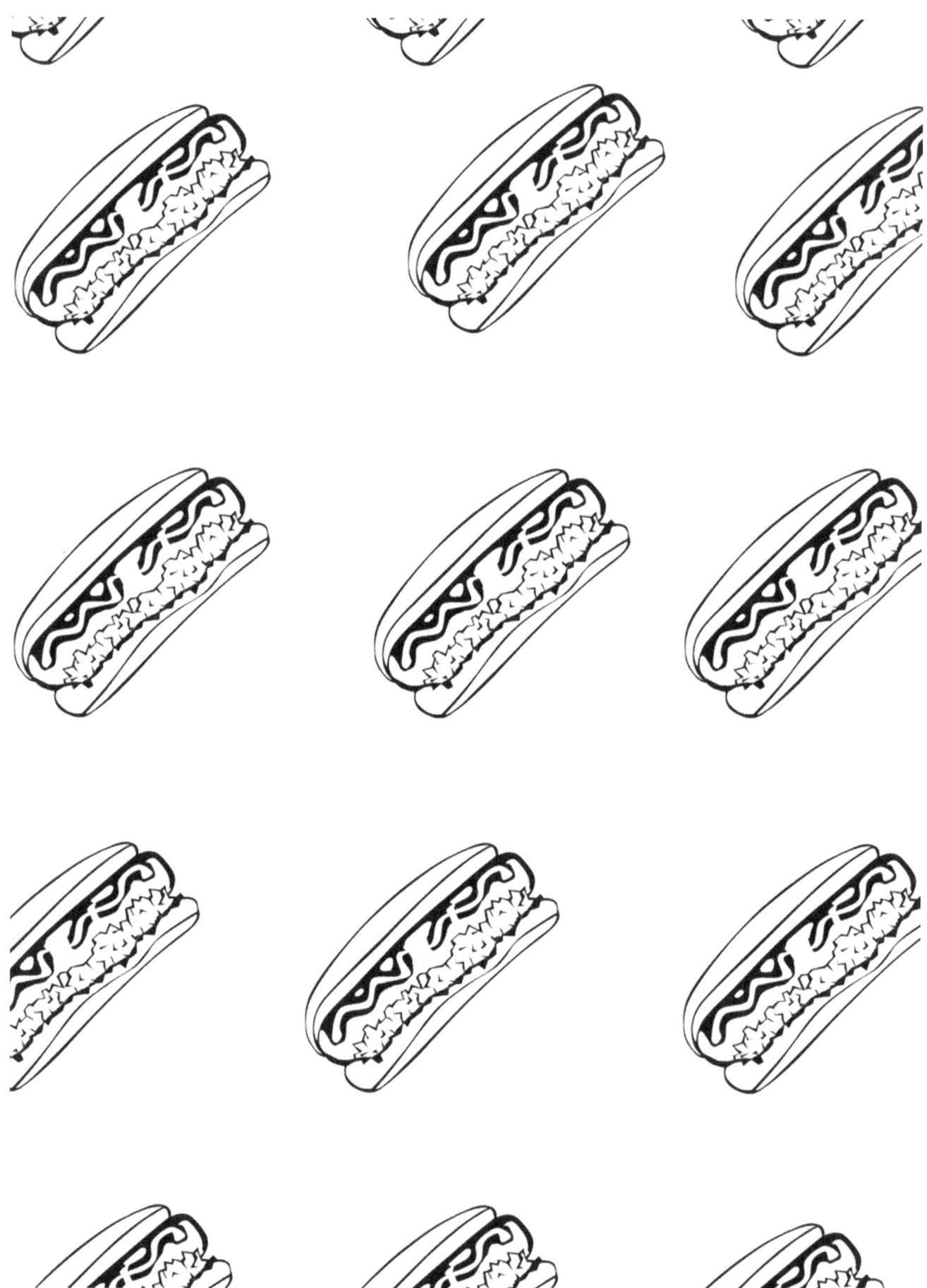

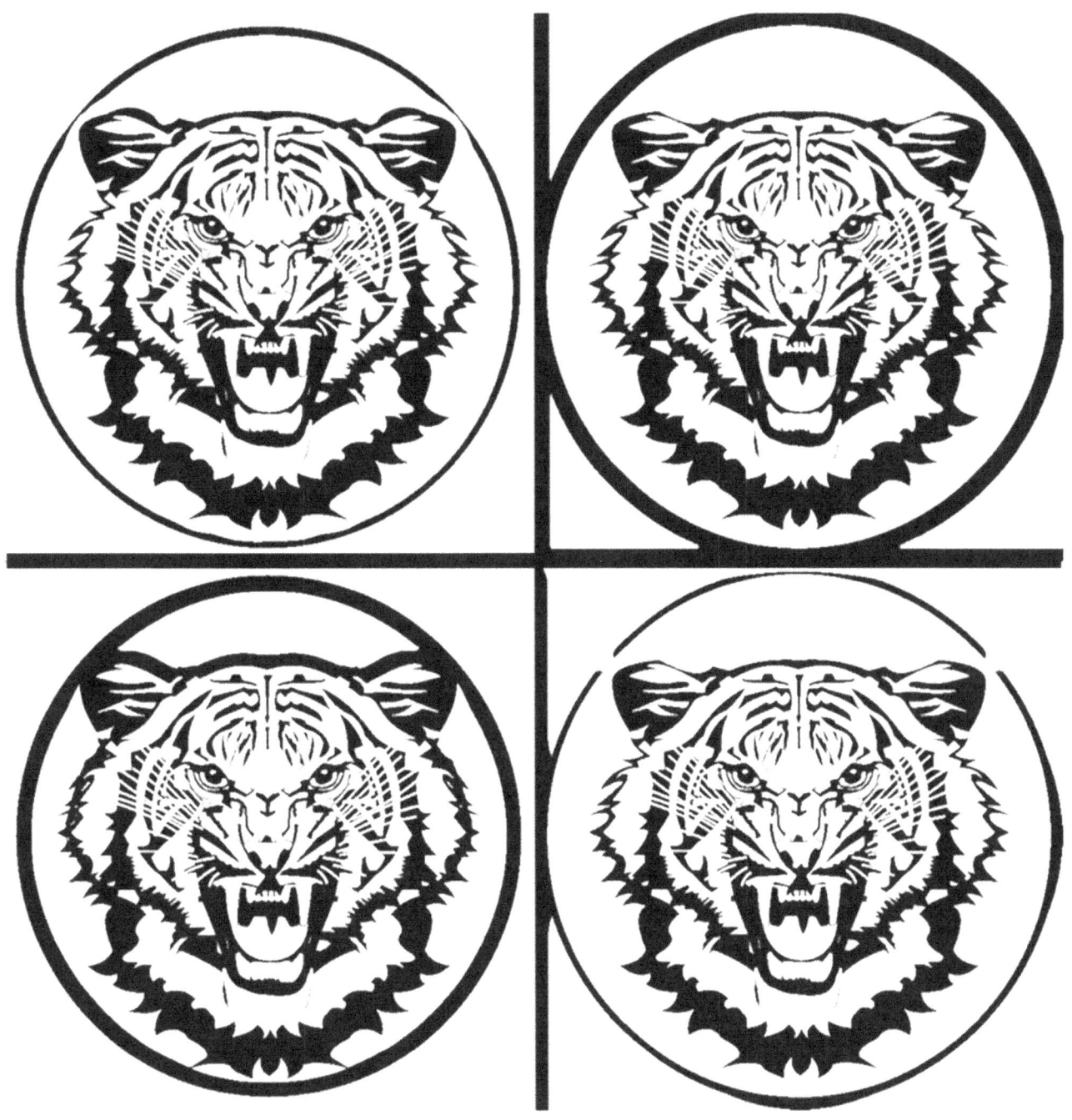

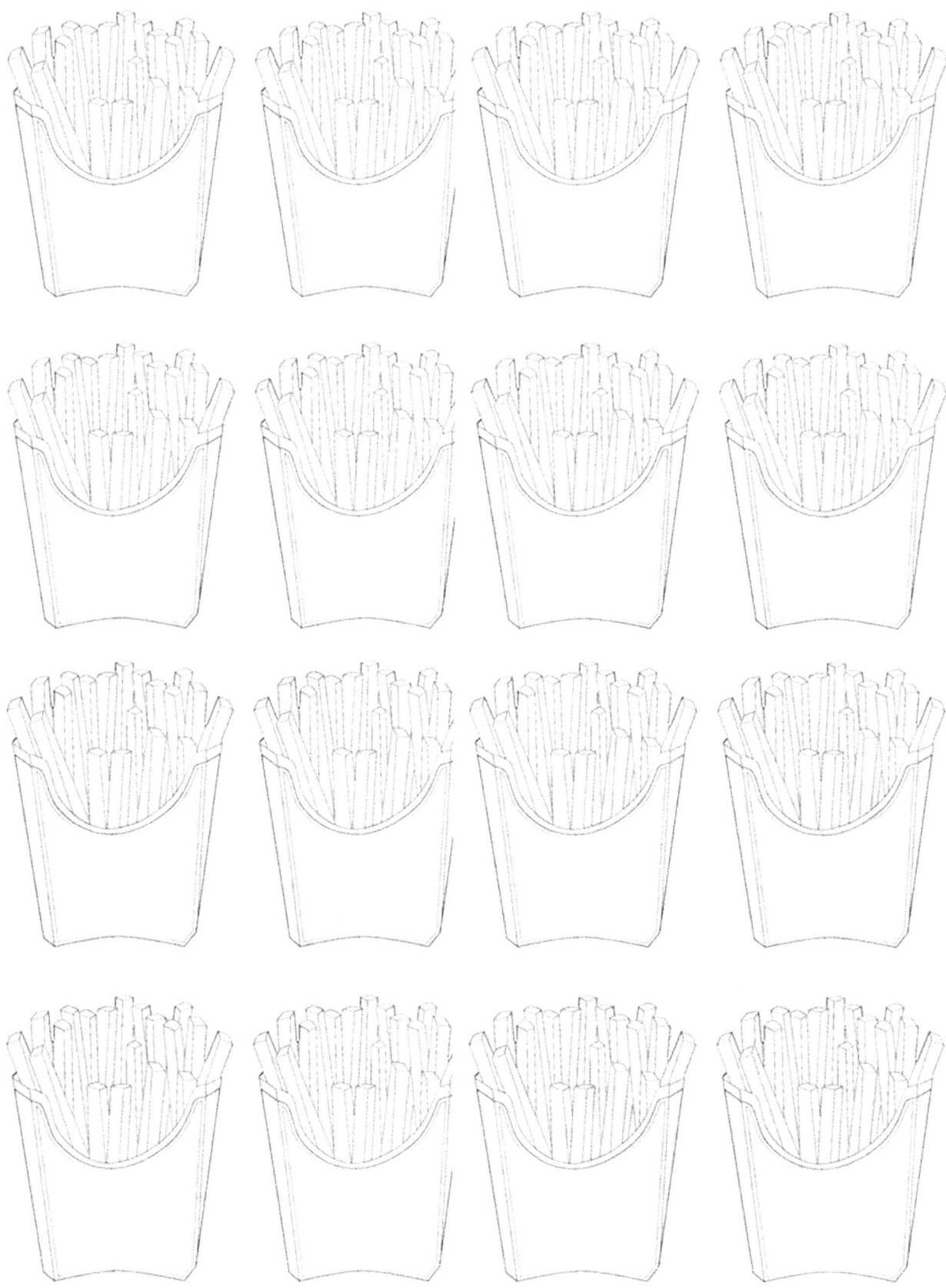

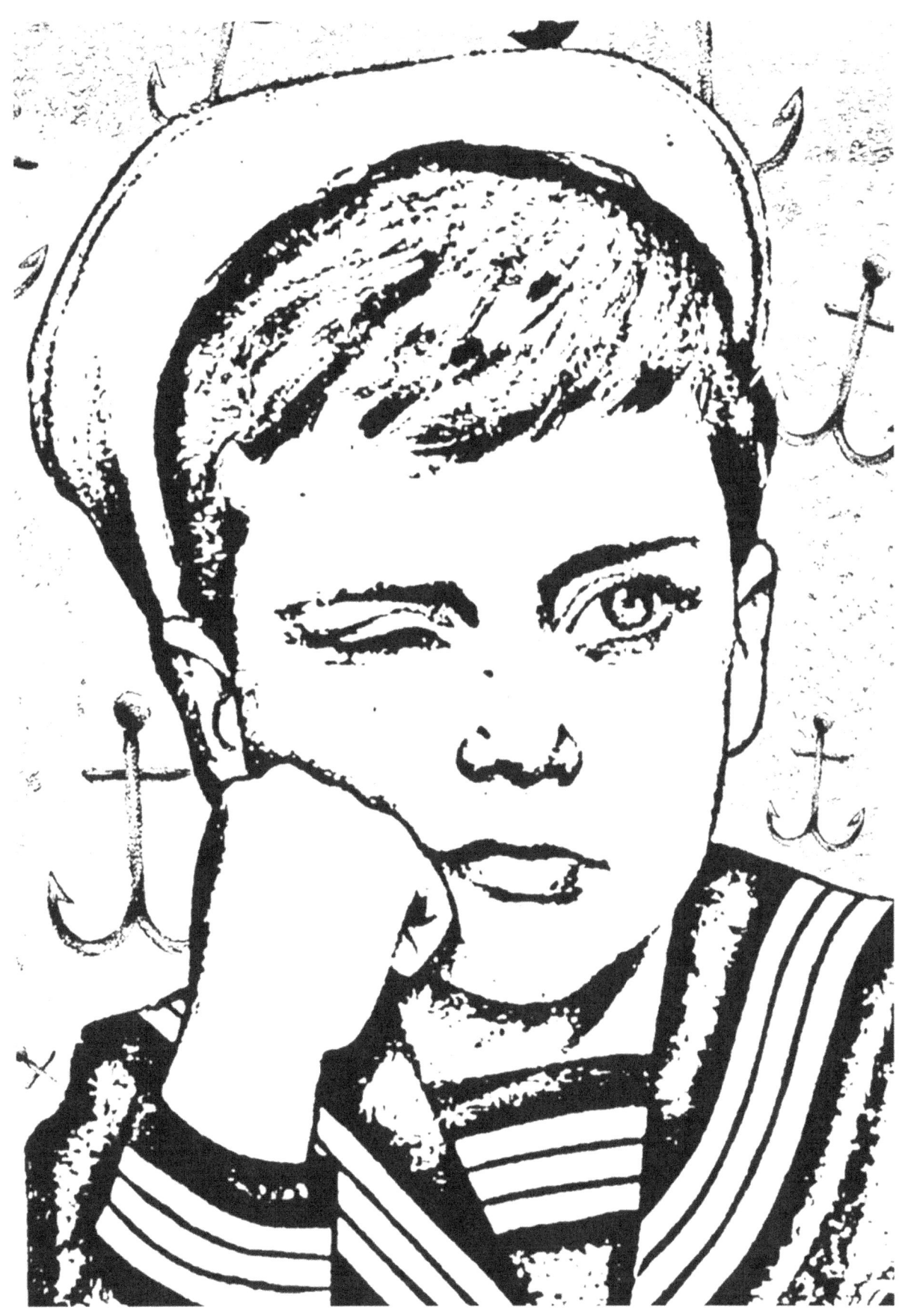

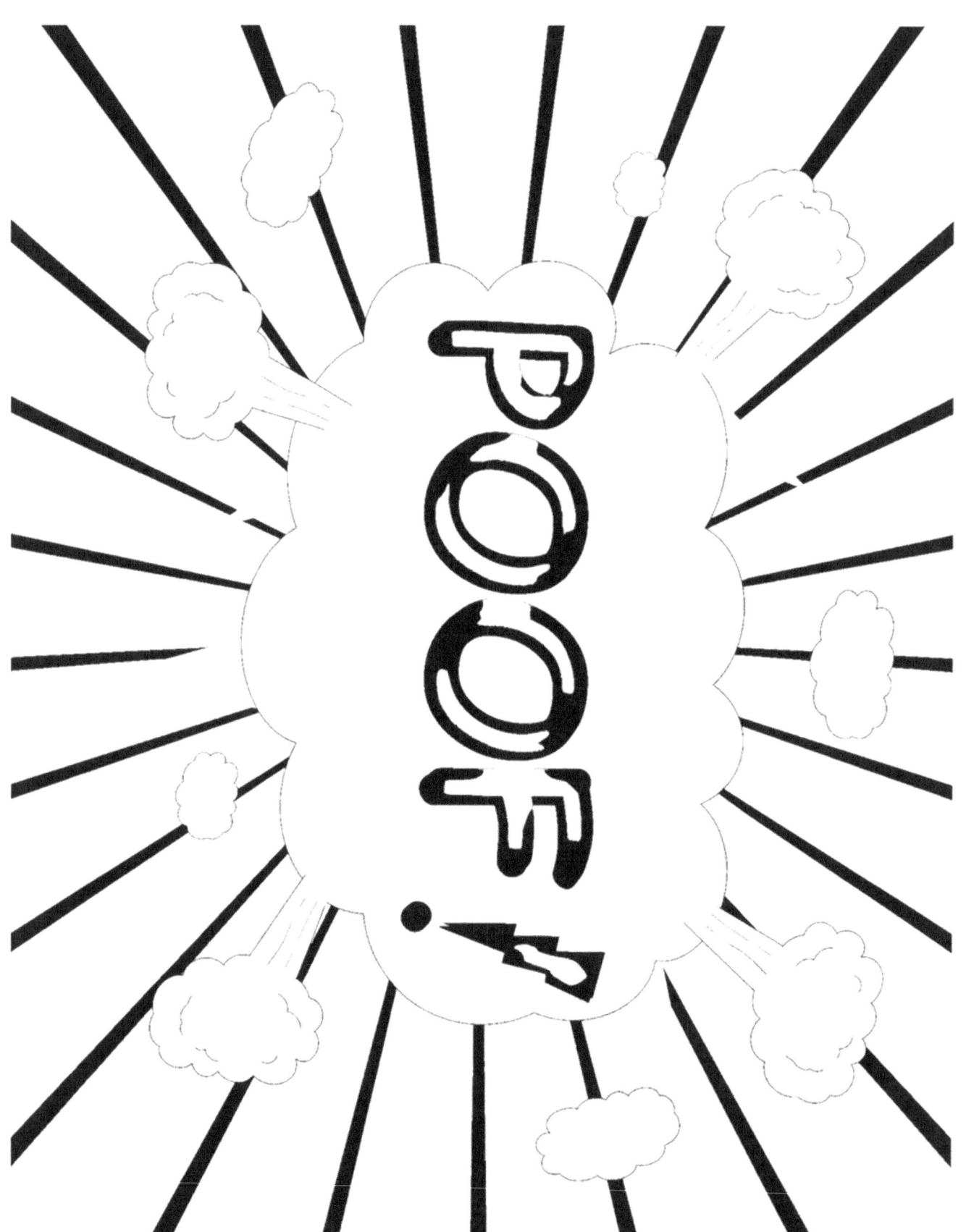

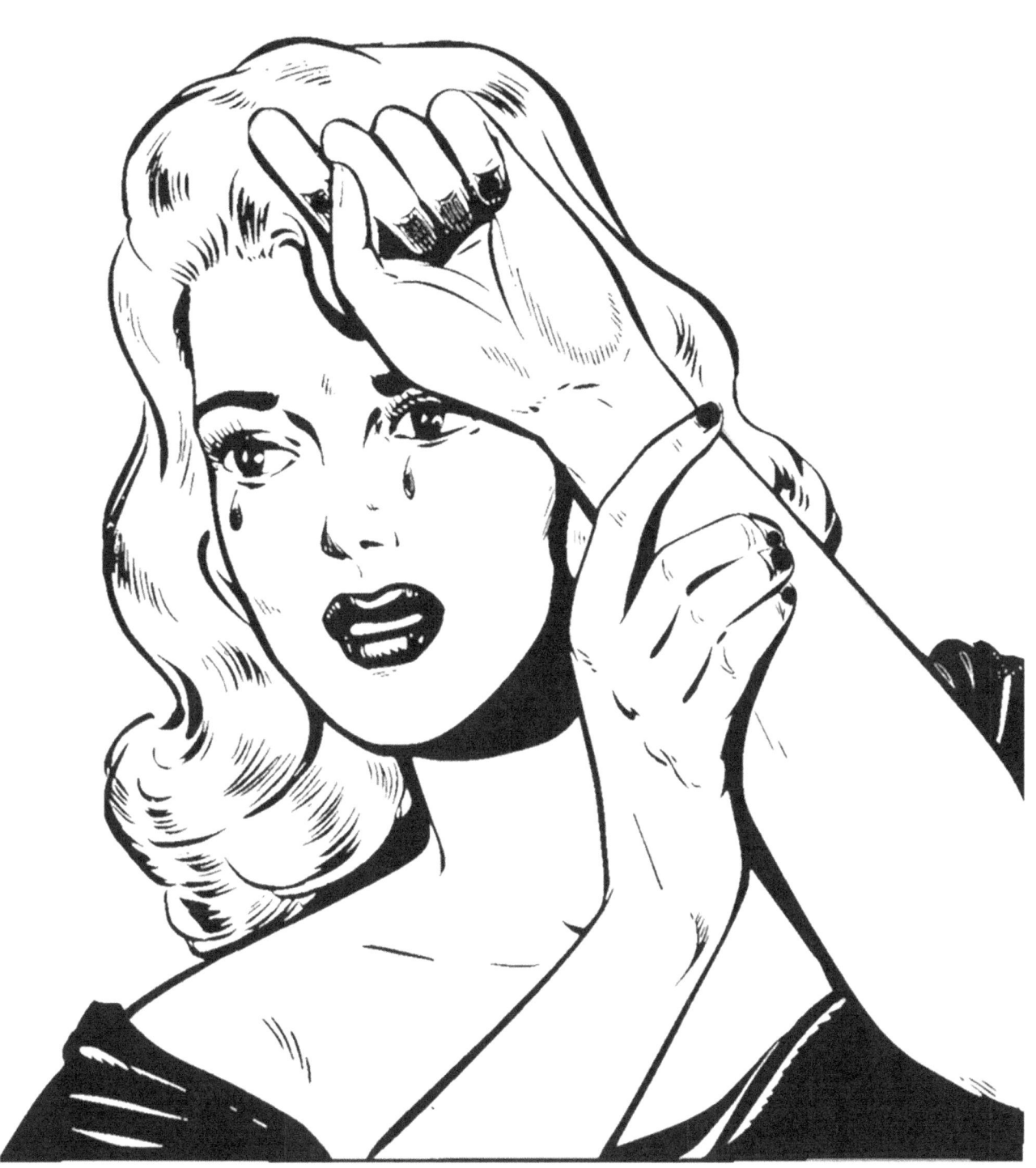

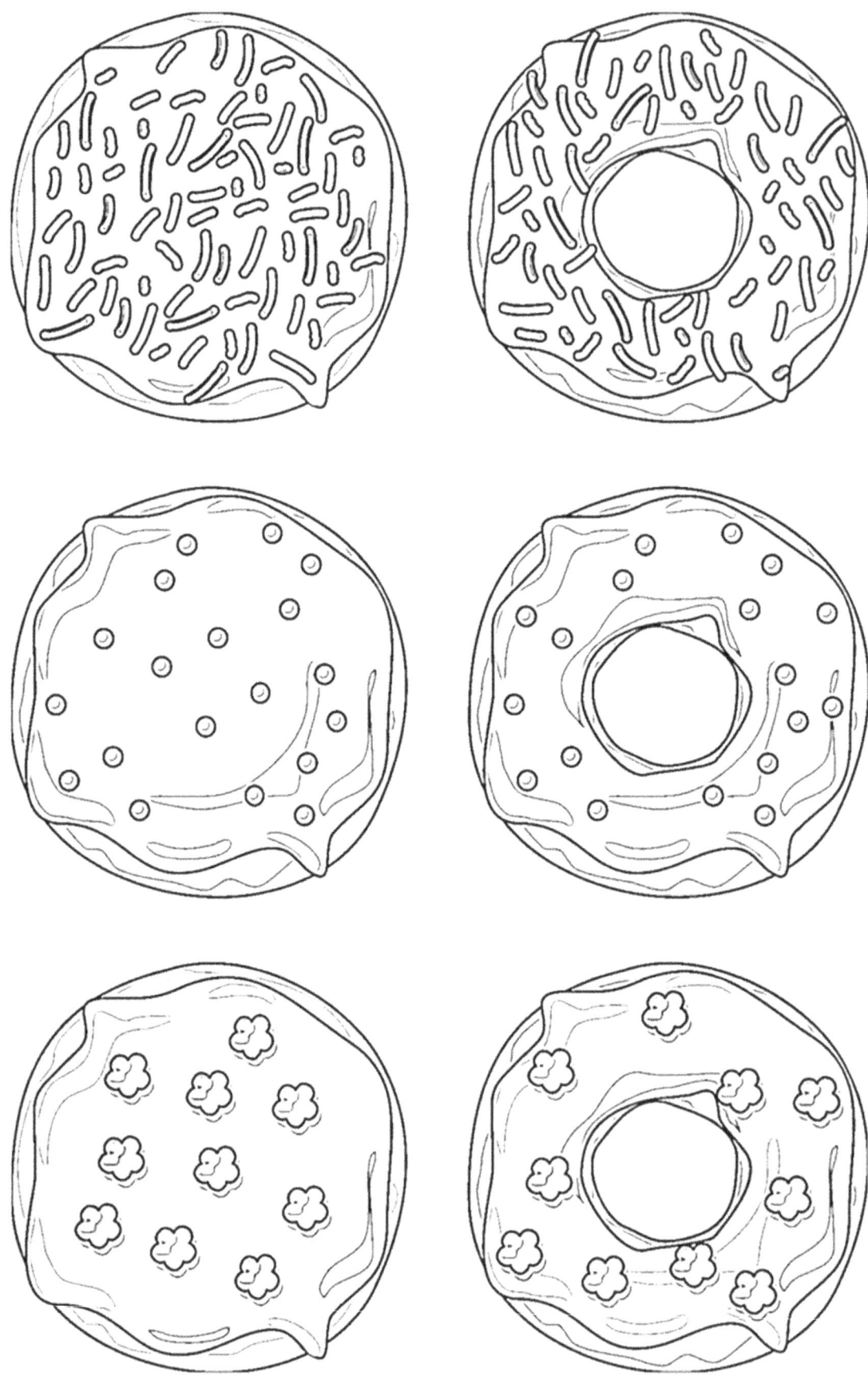

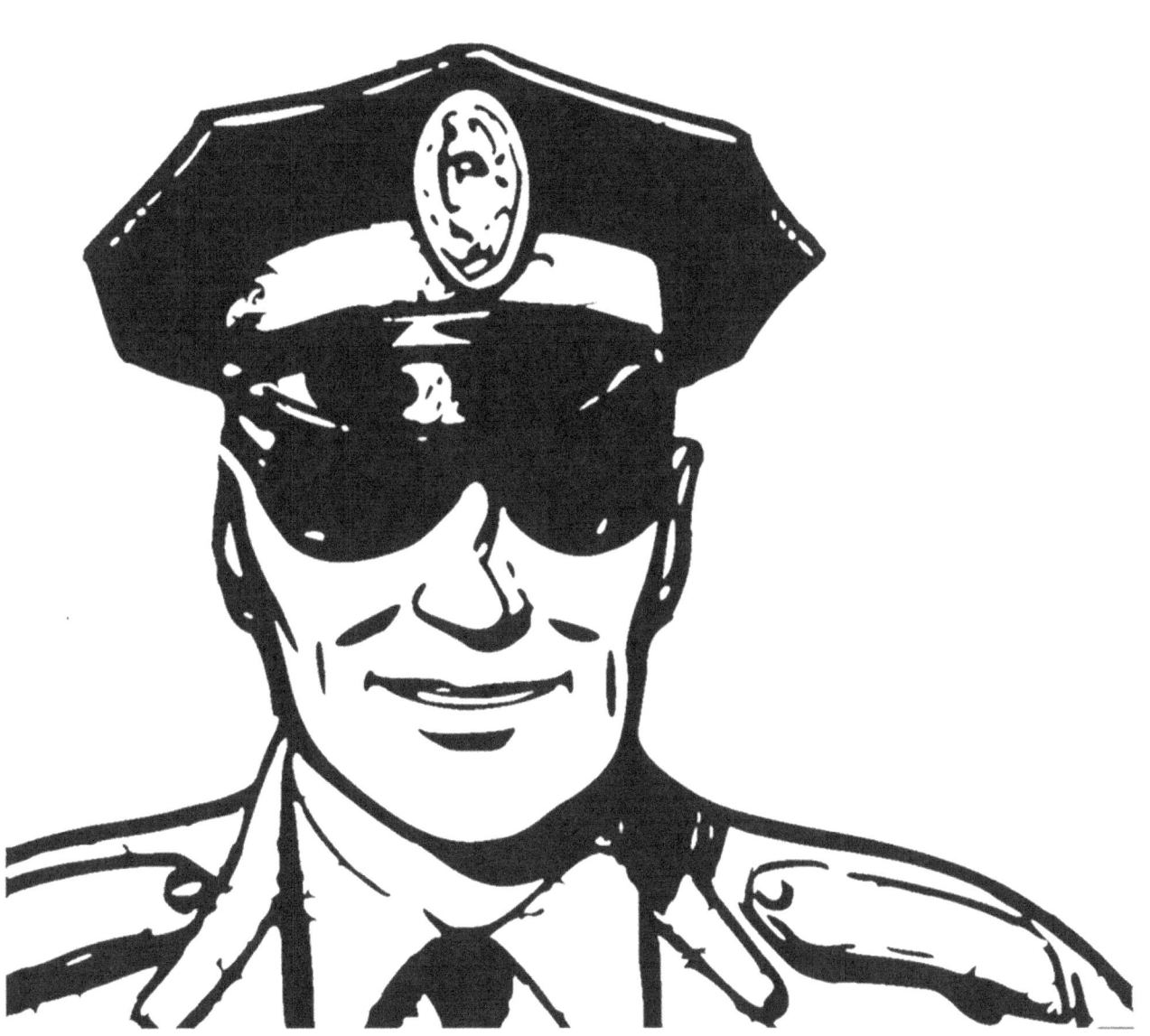

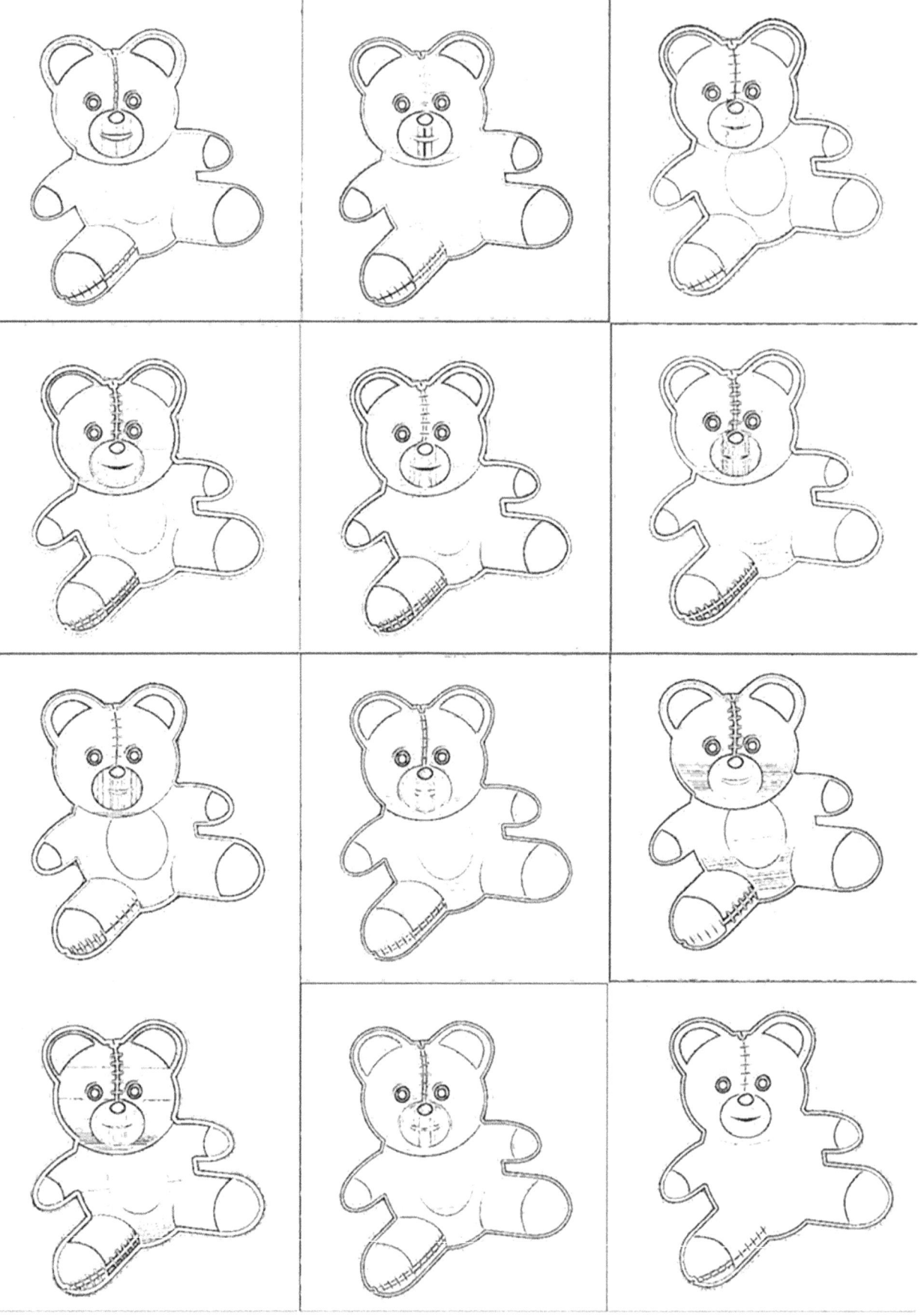

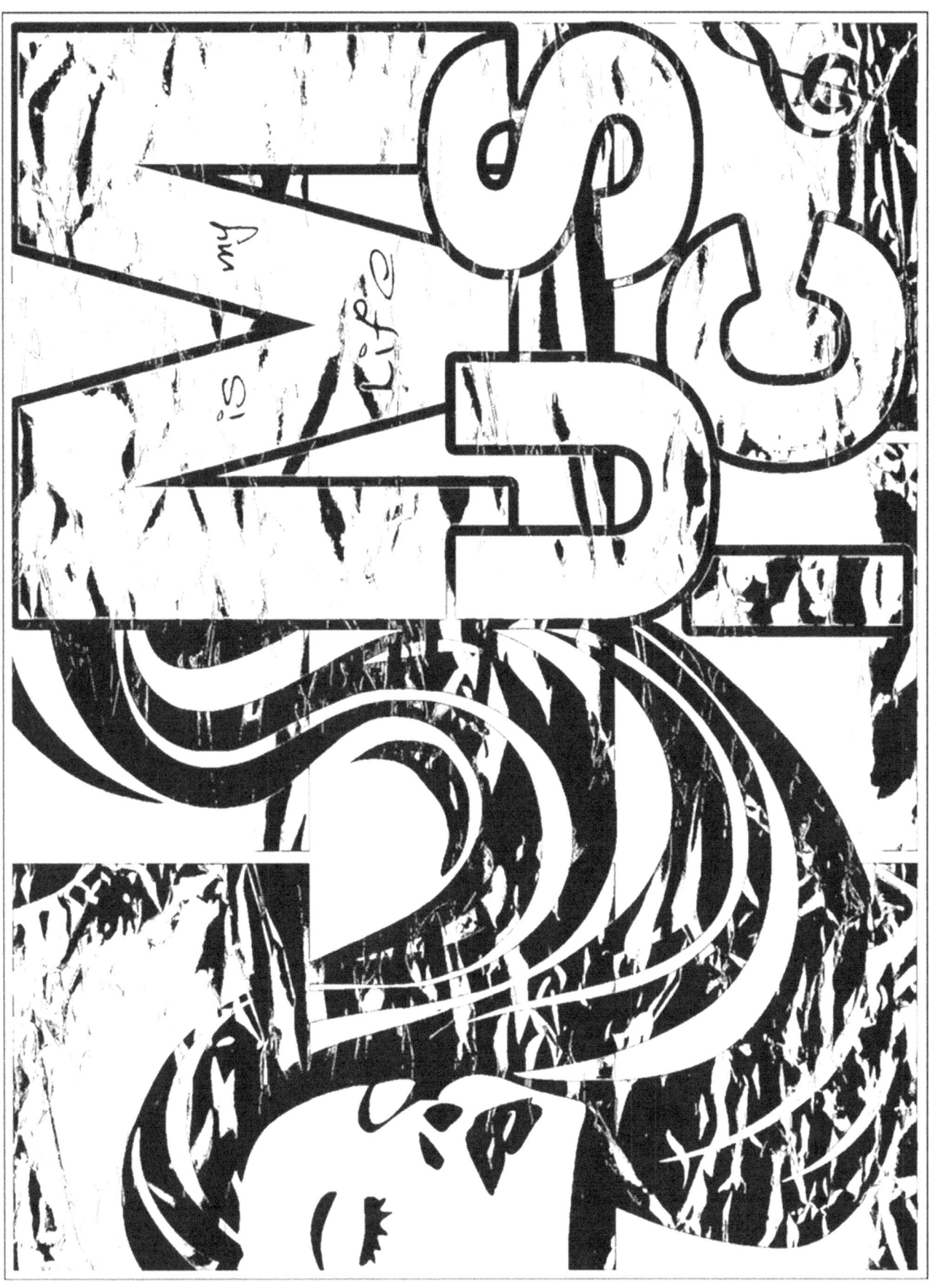

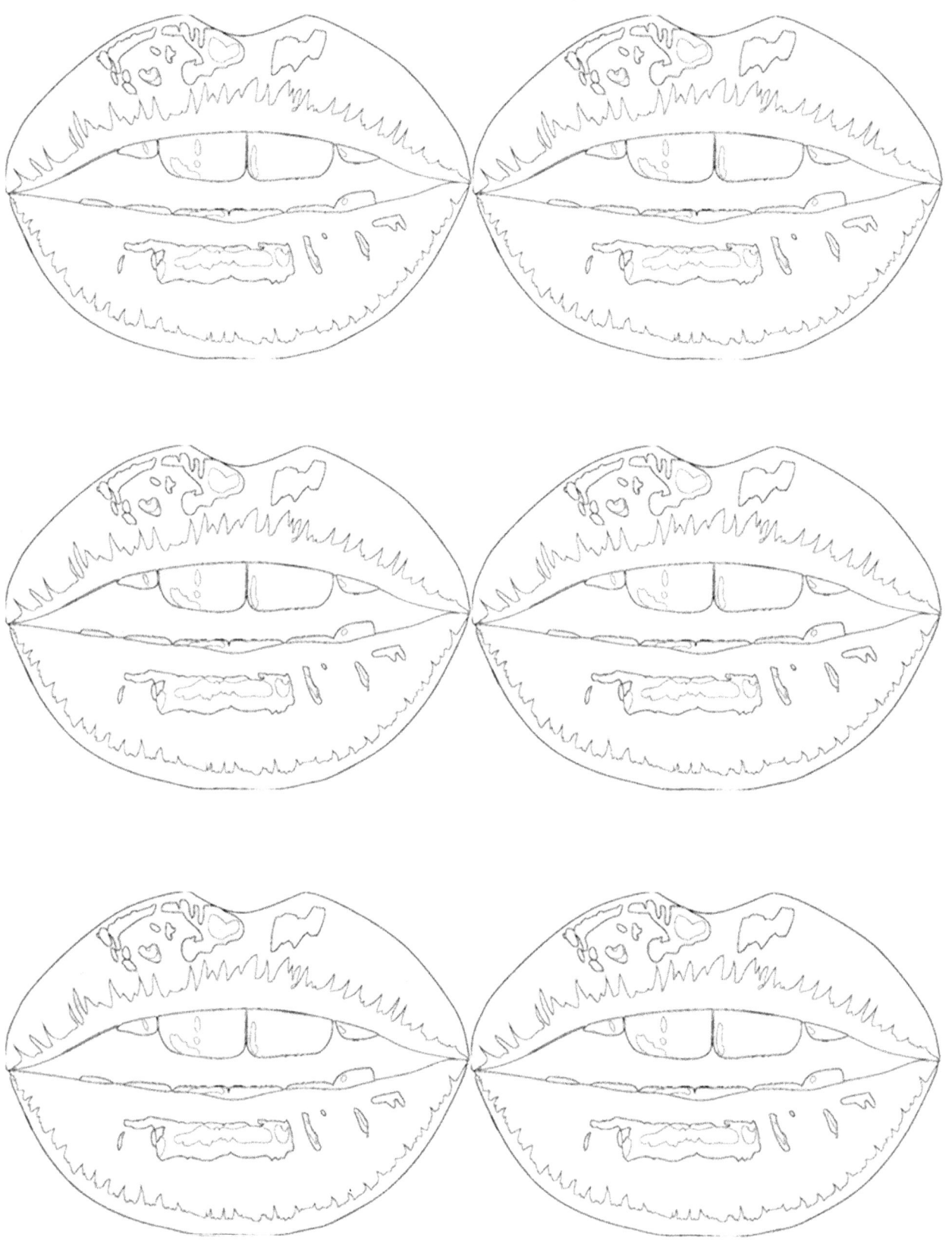

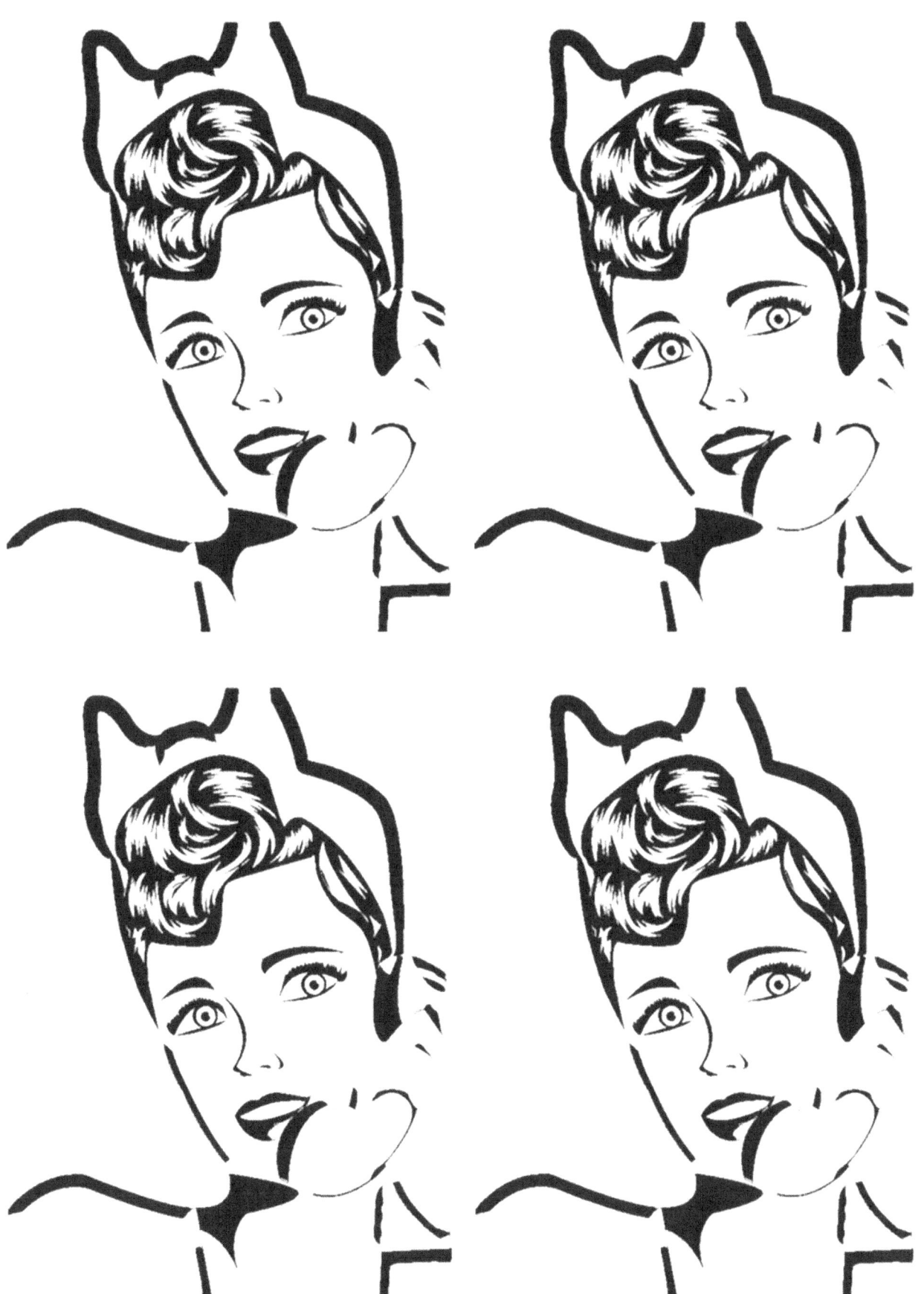

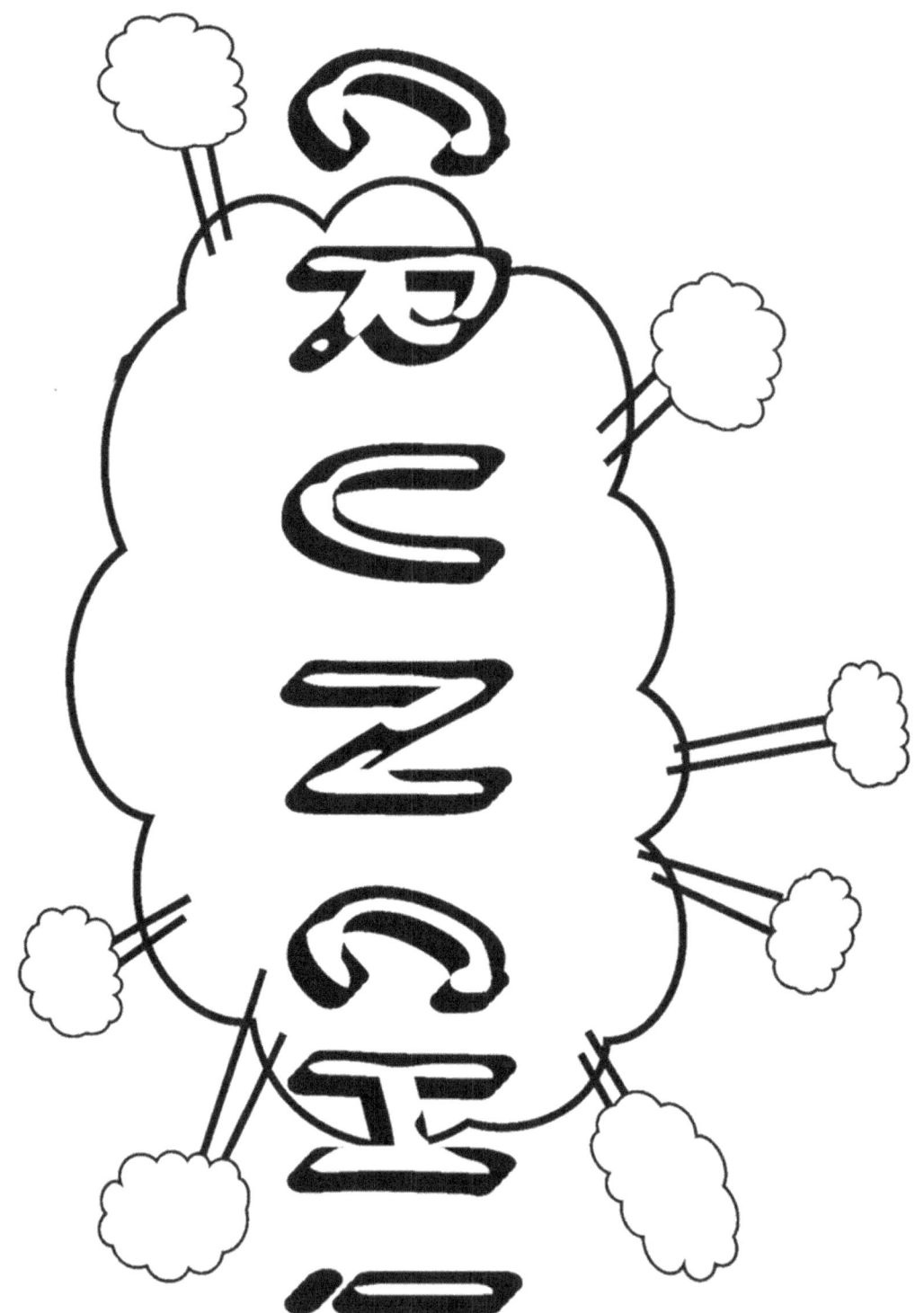

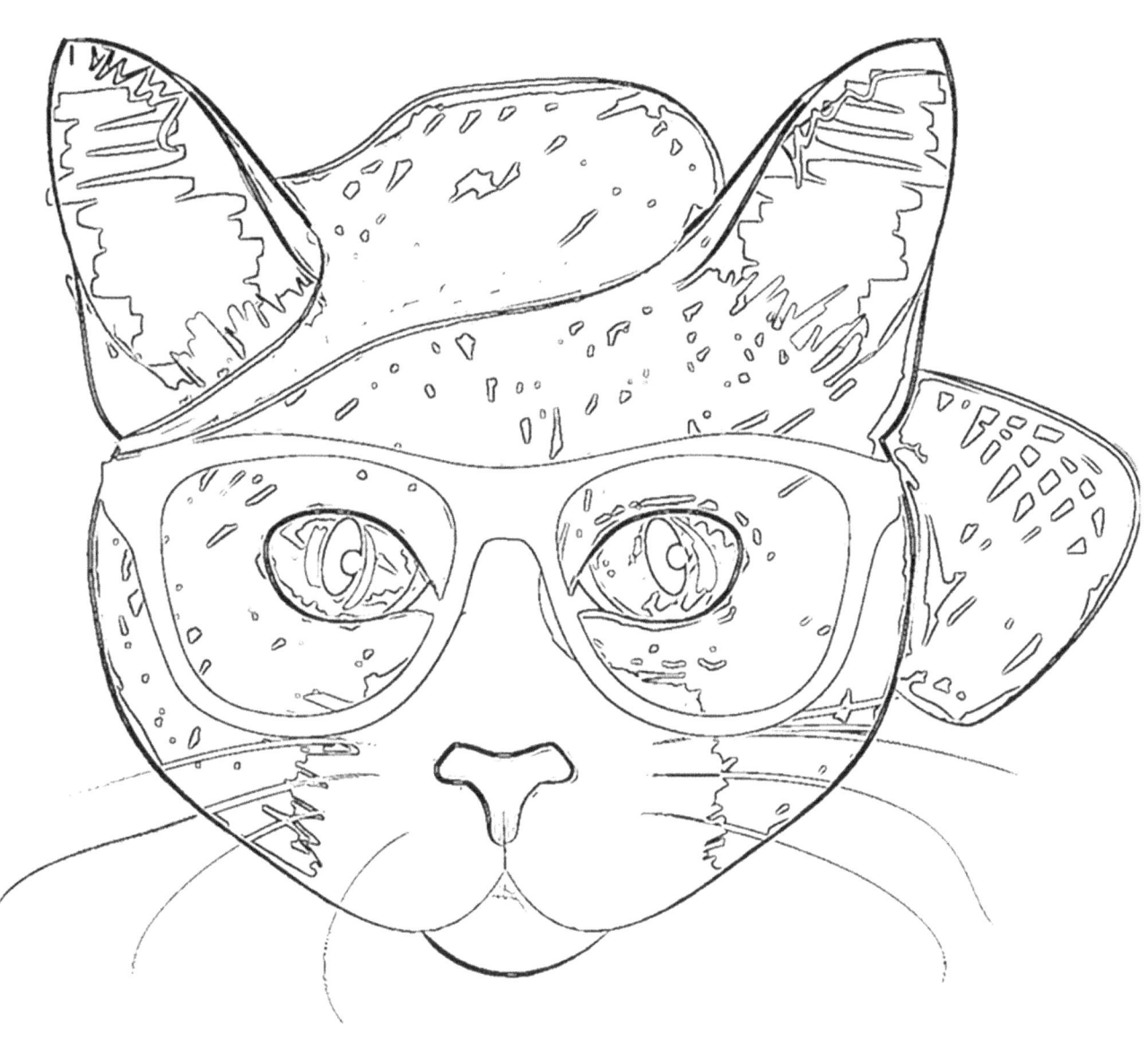

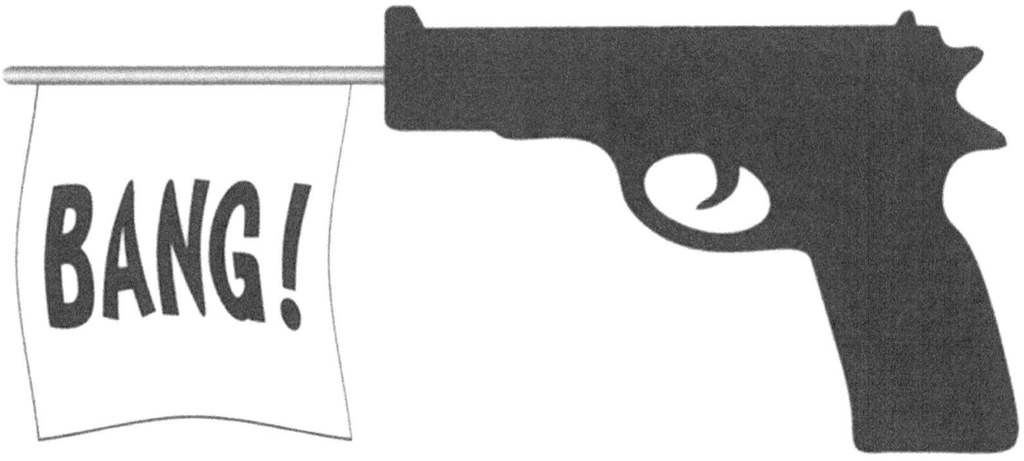
BANG!

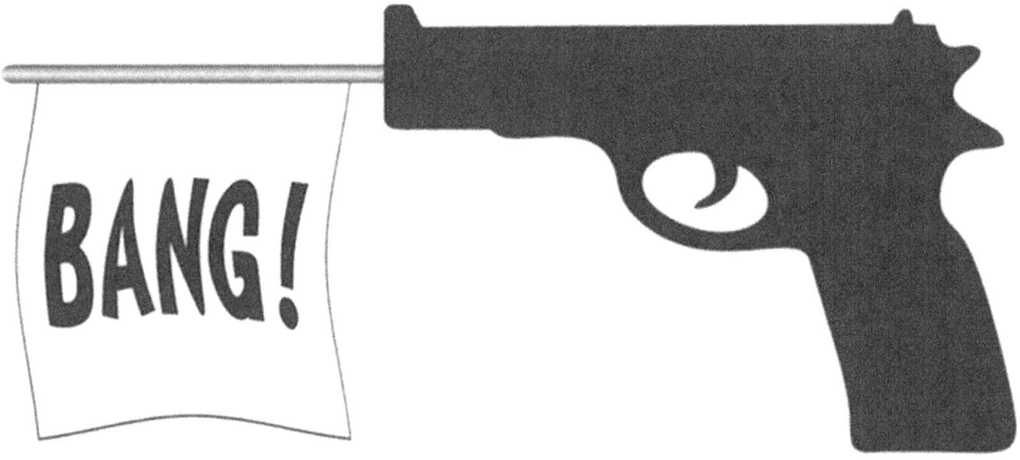
BANG!

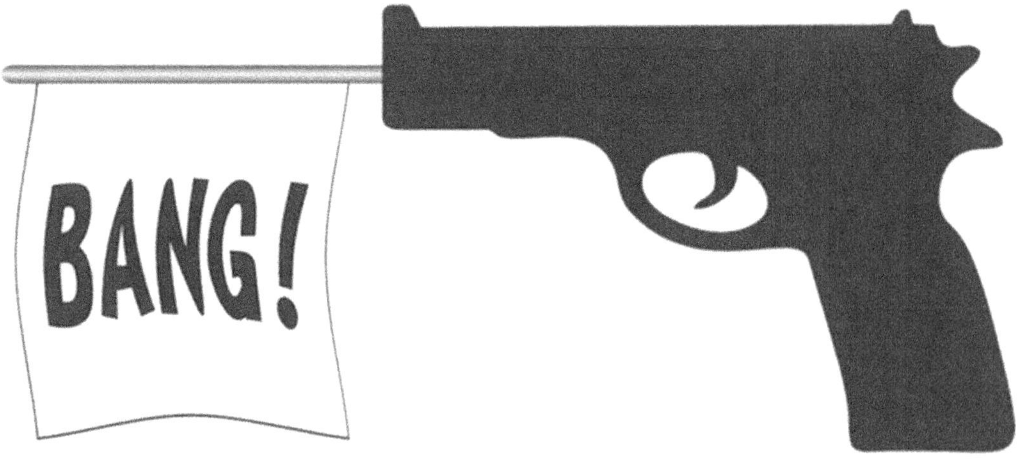
BANG!

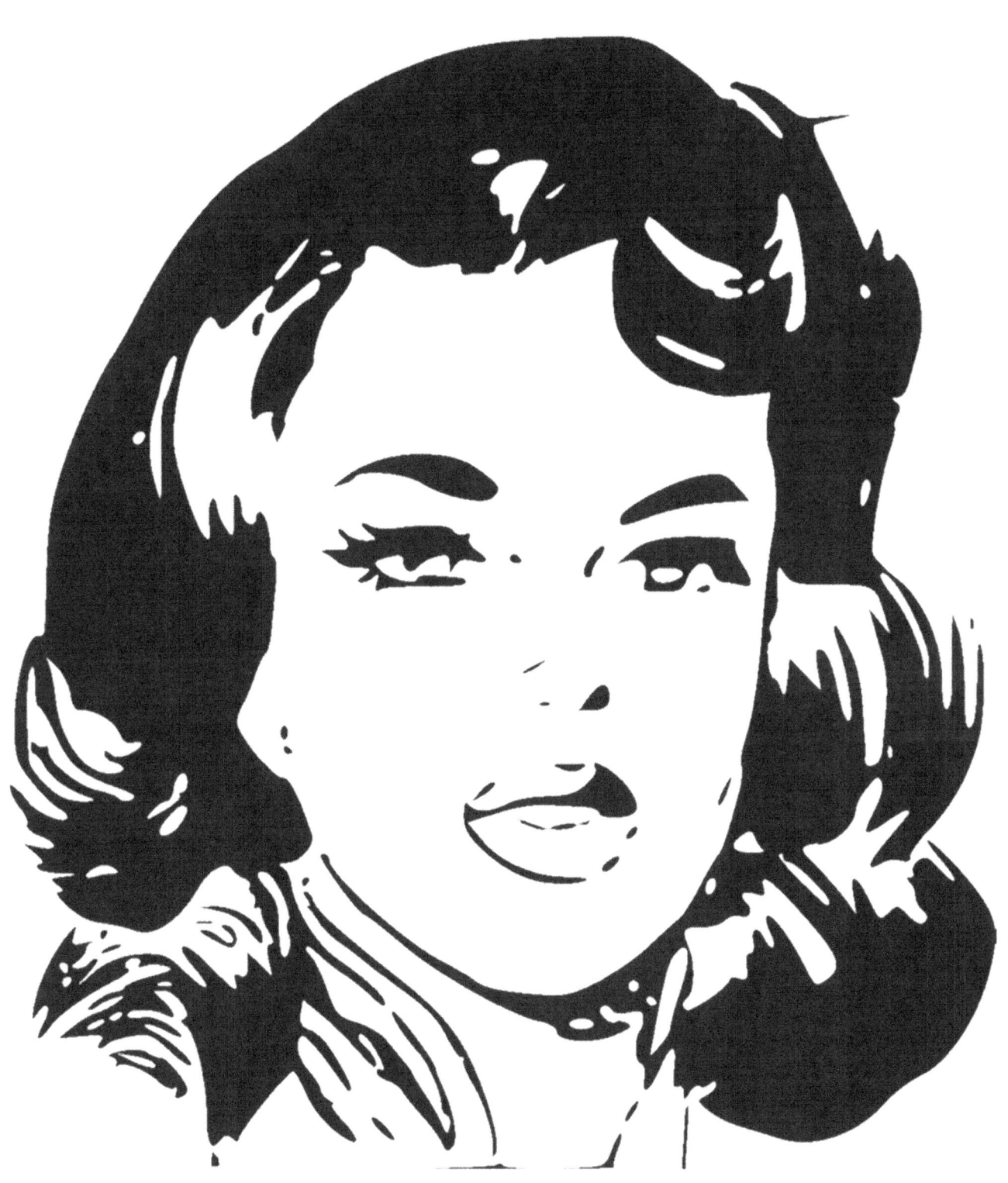

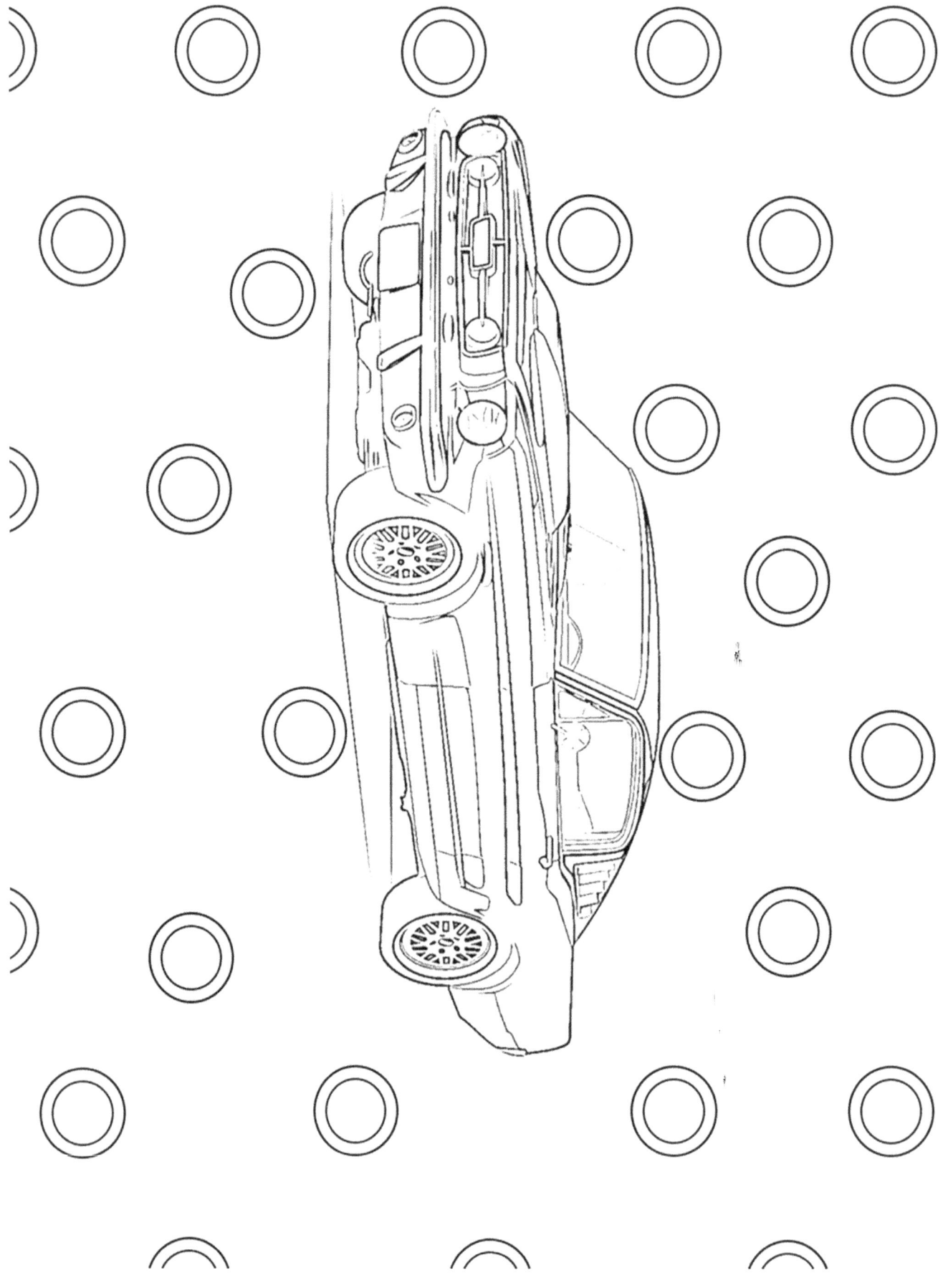

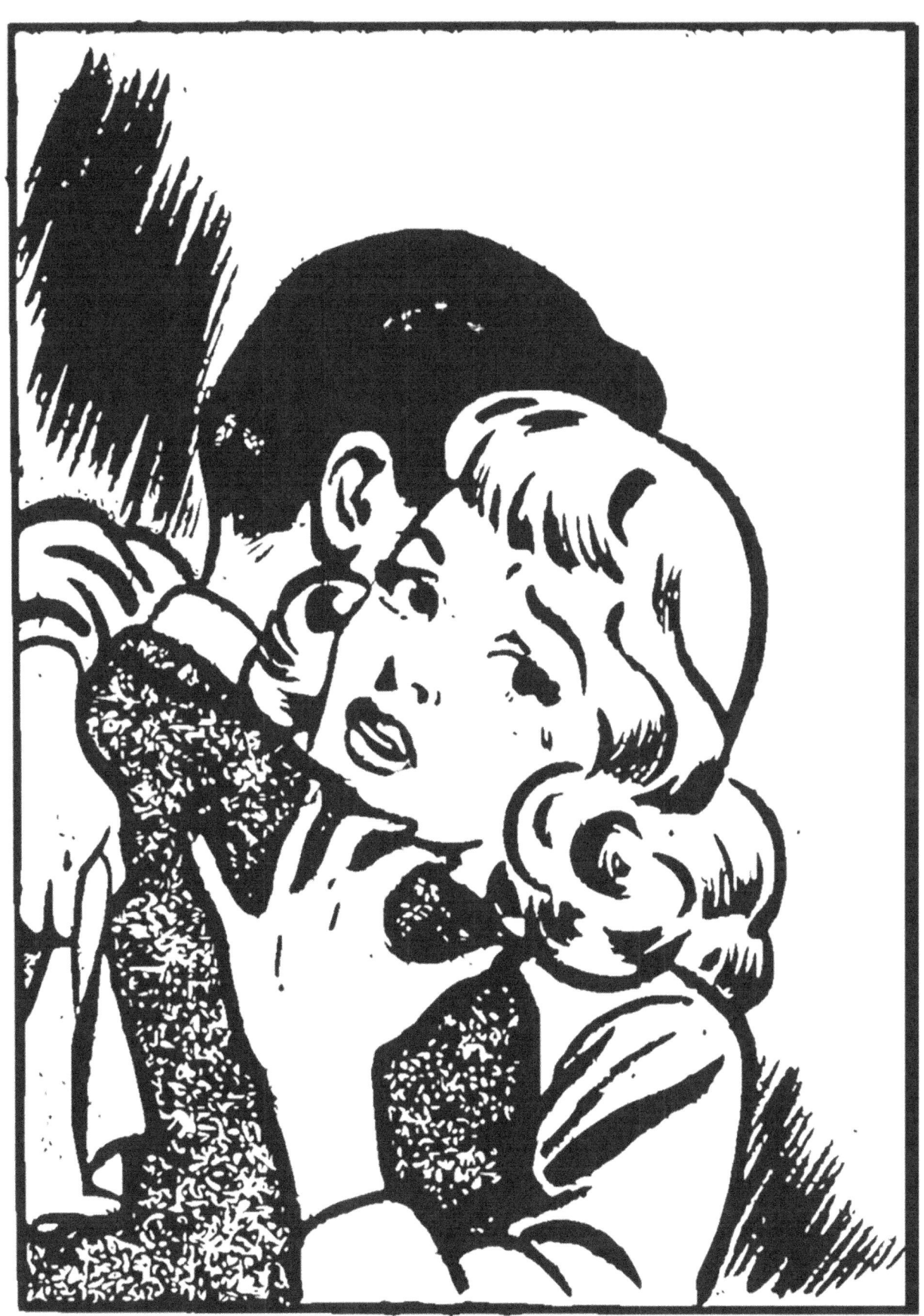

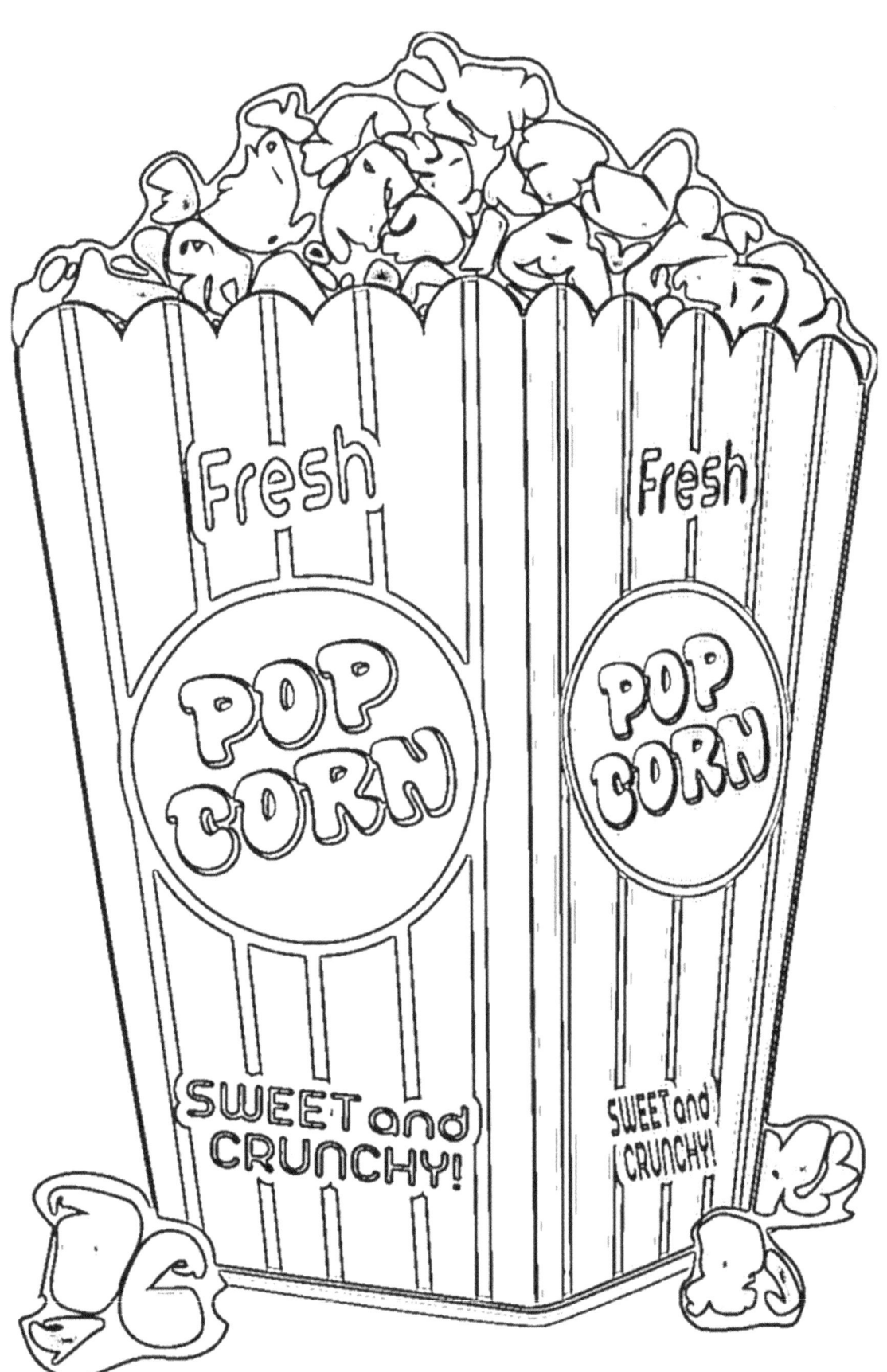

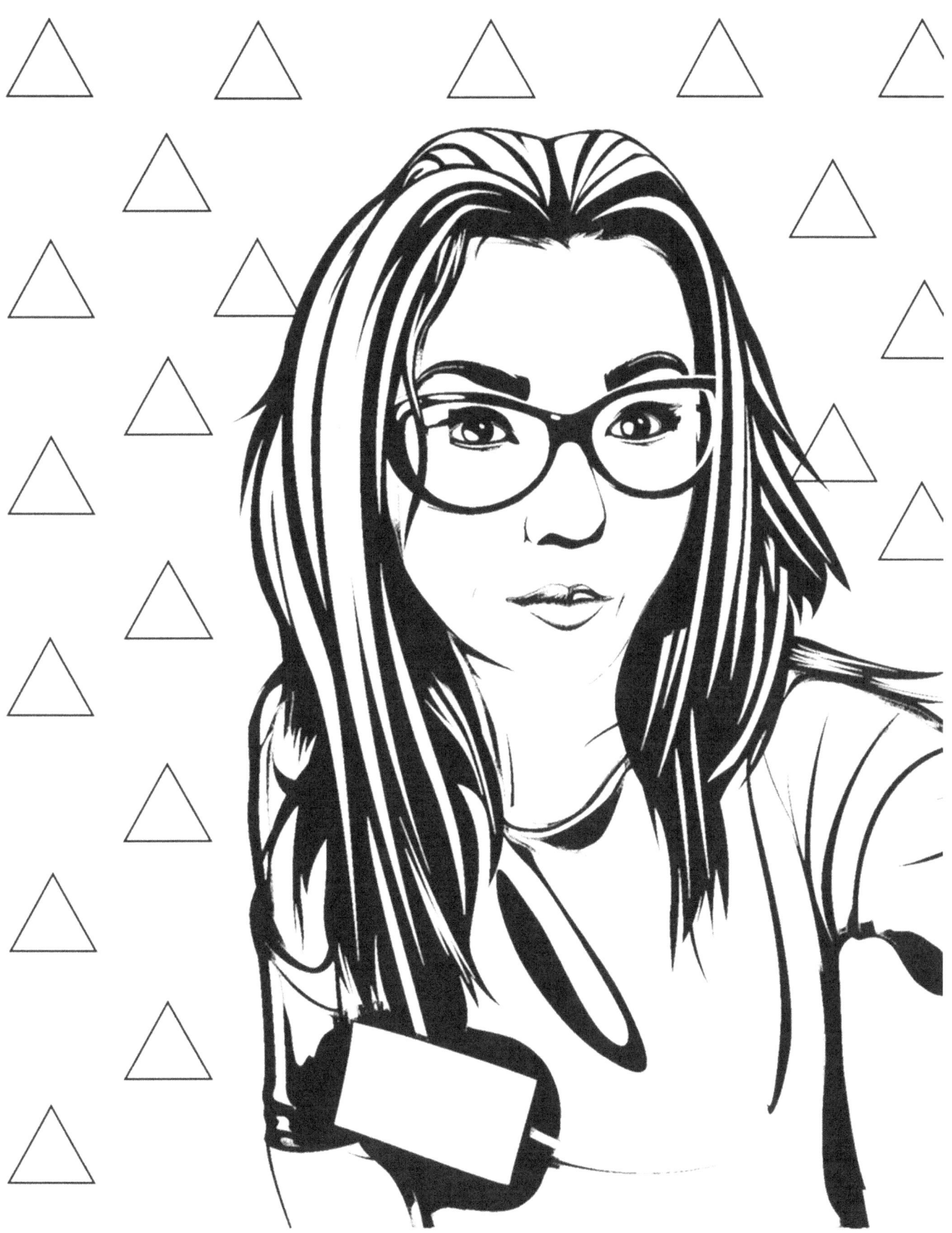

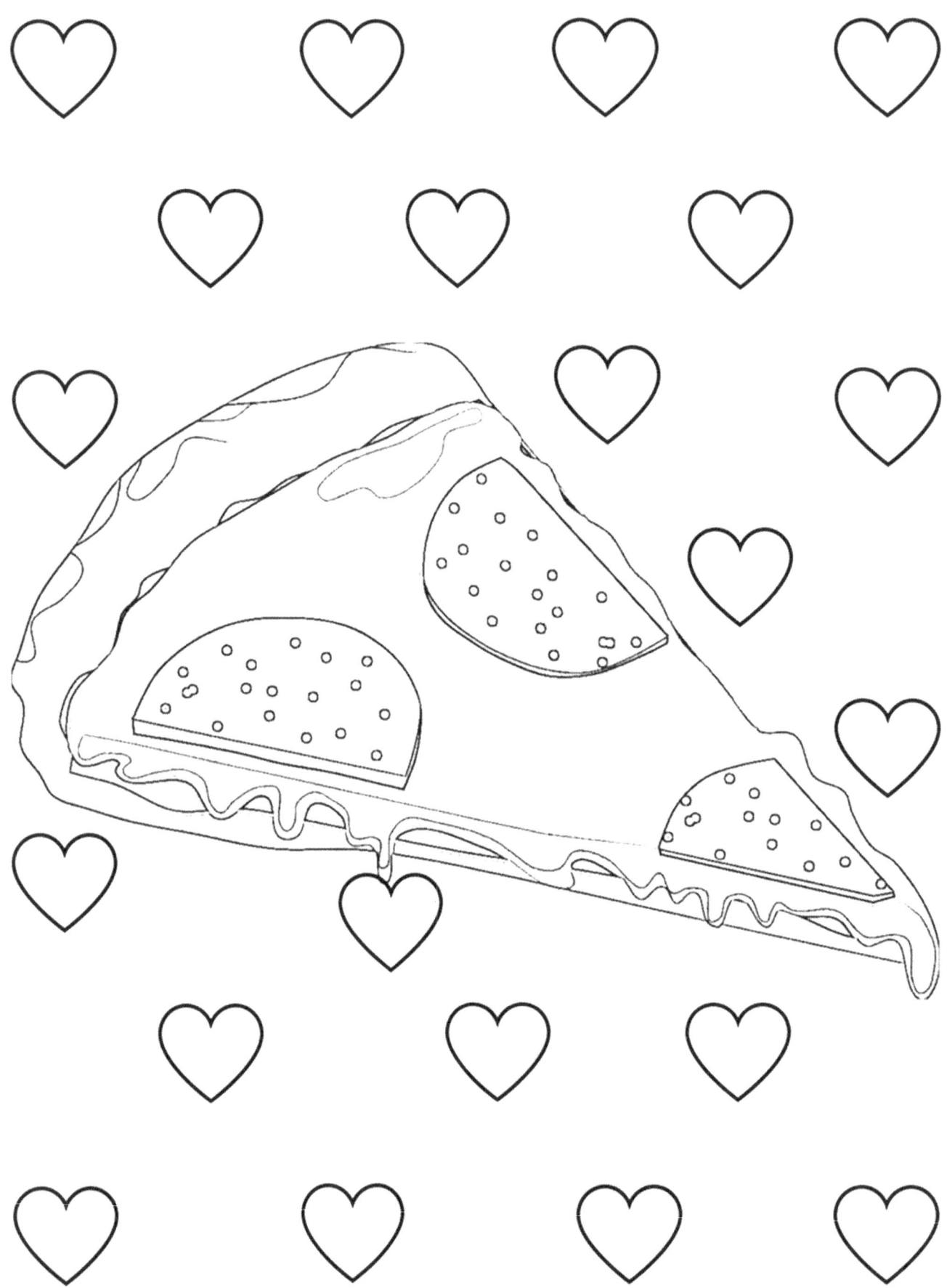

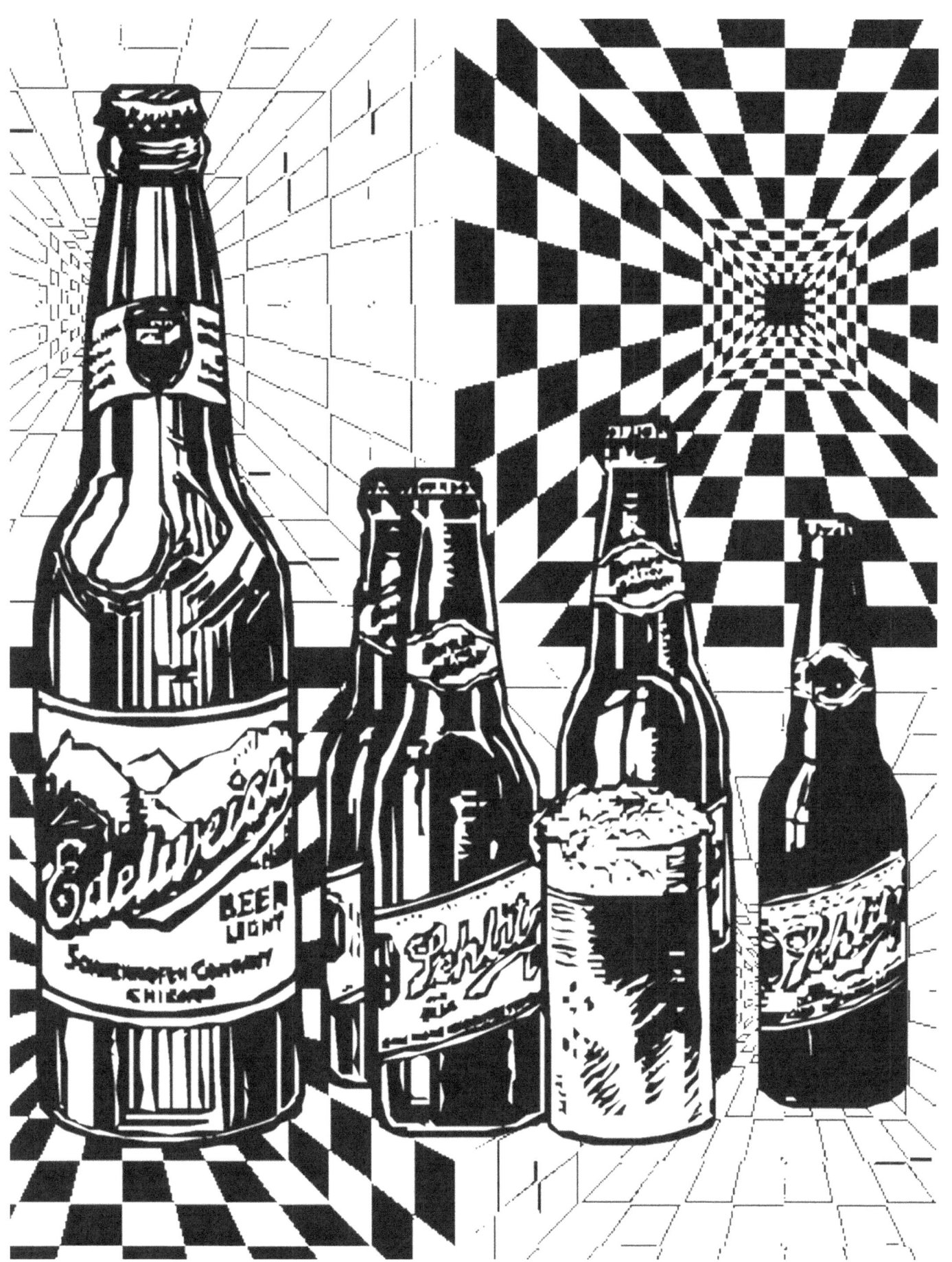

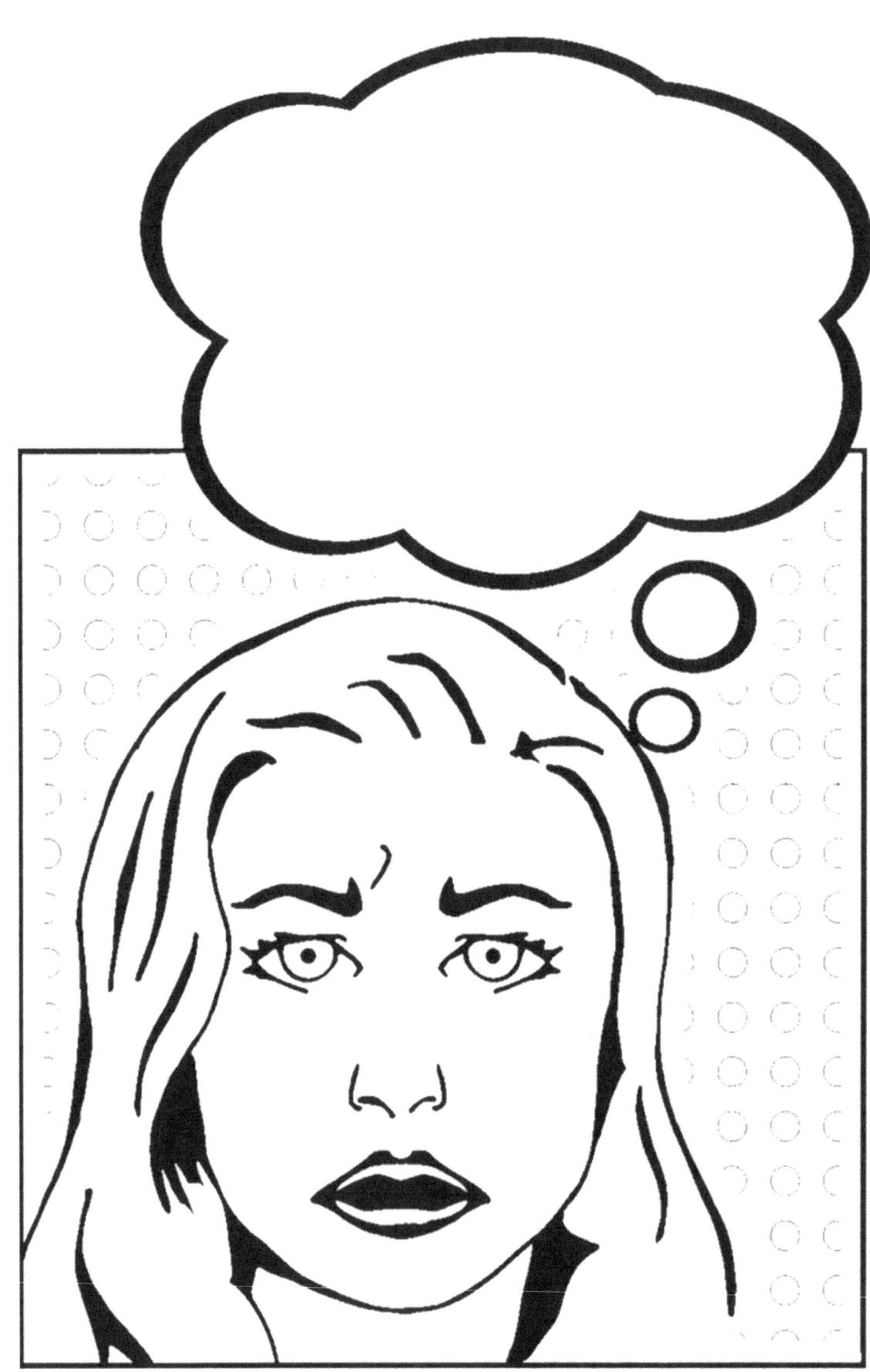

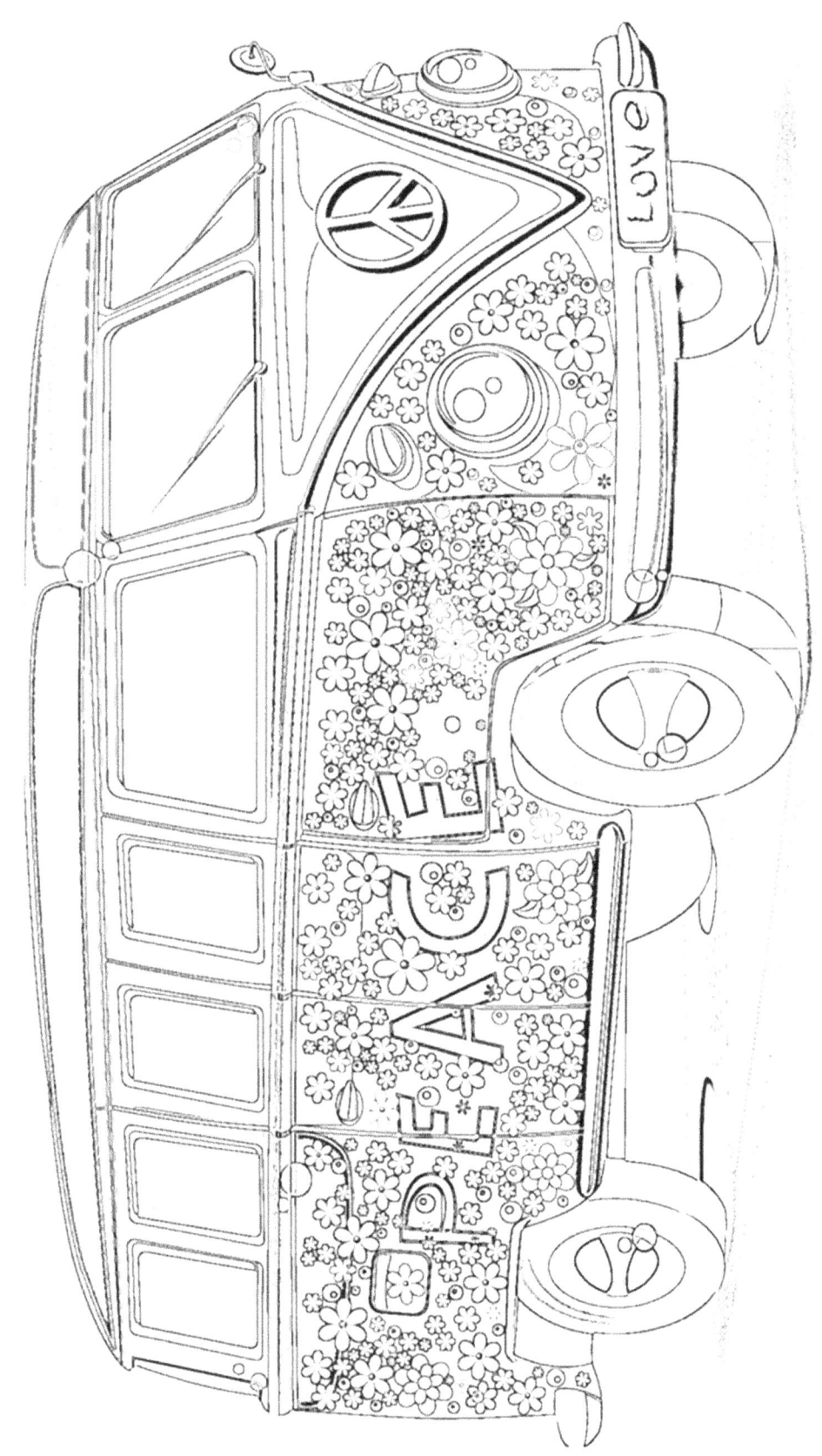

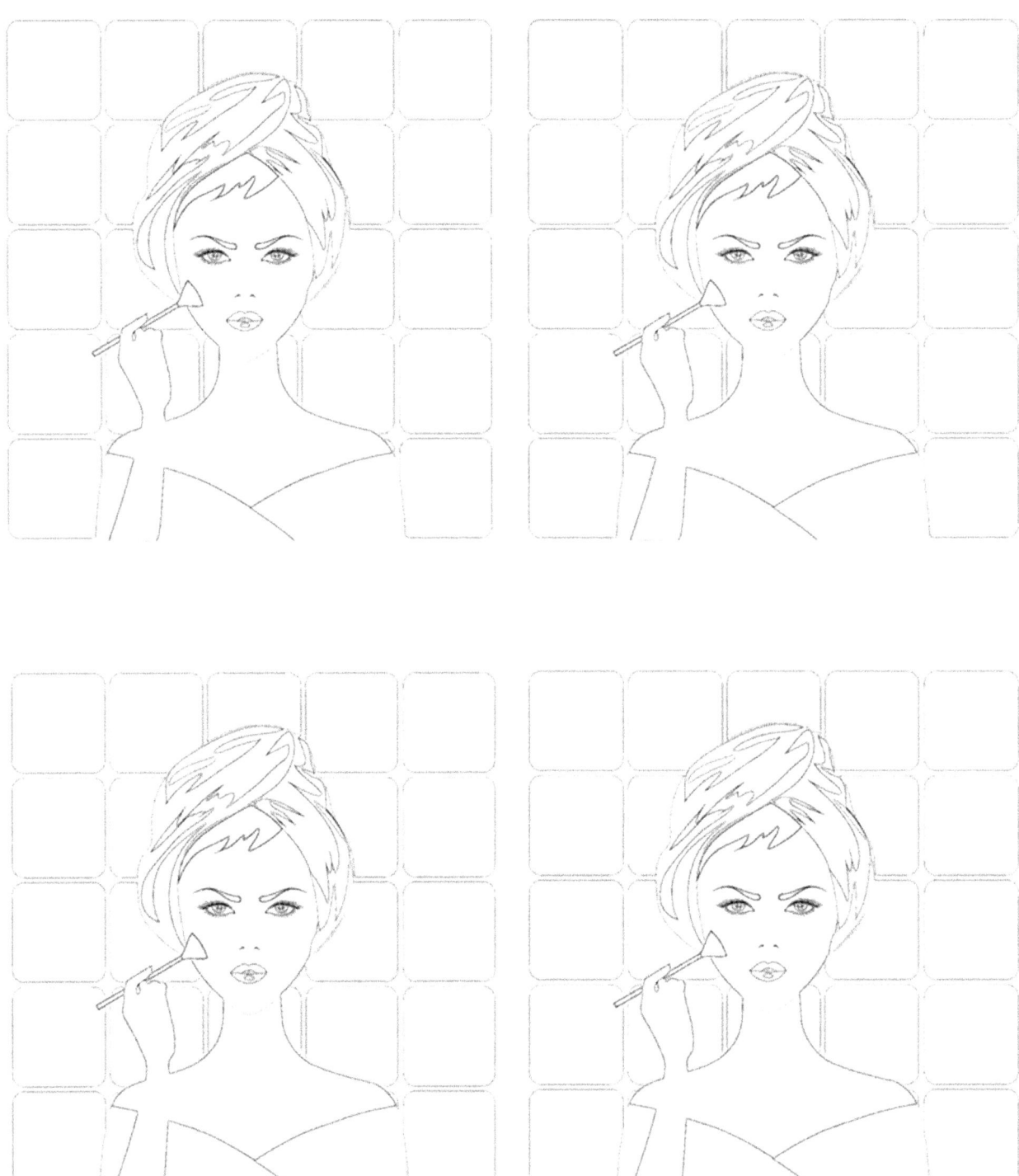

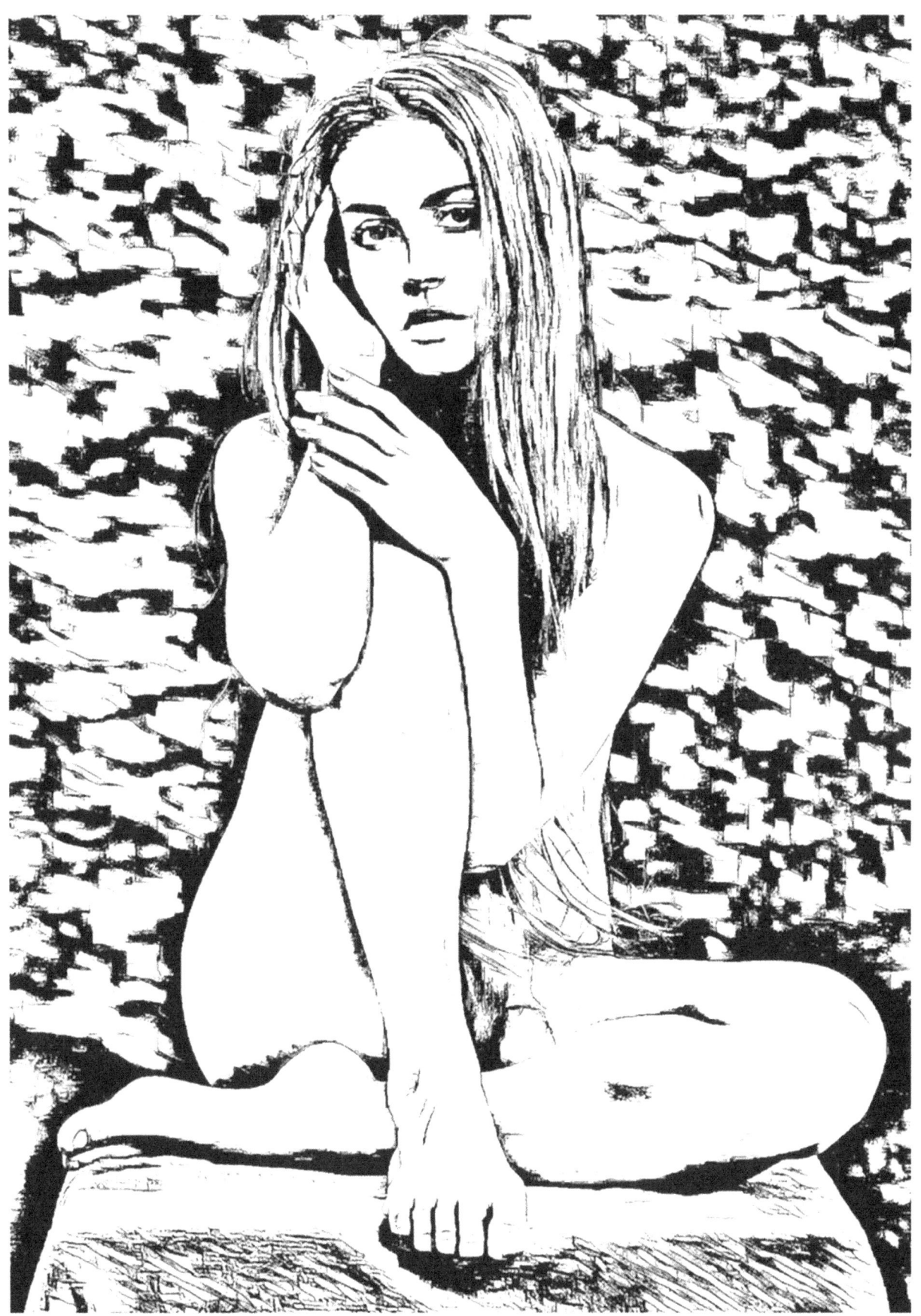

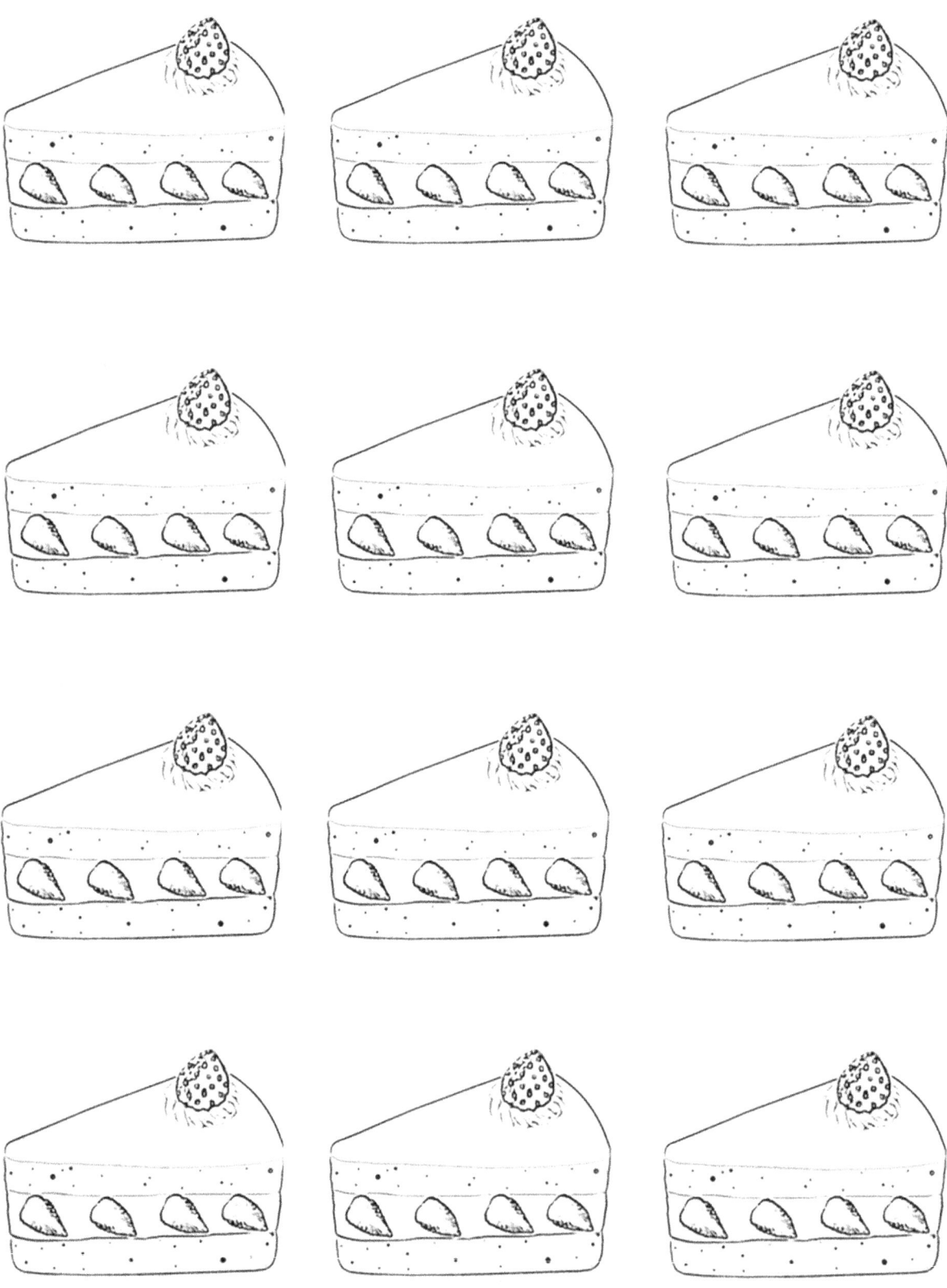

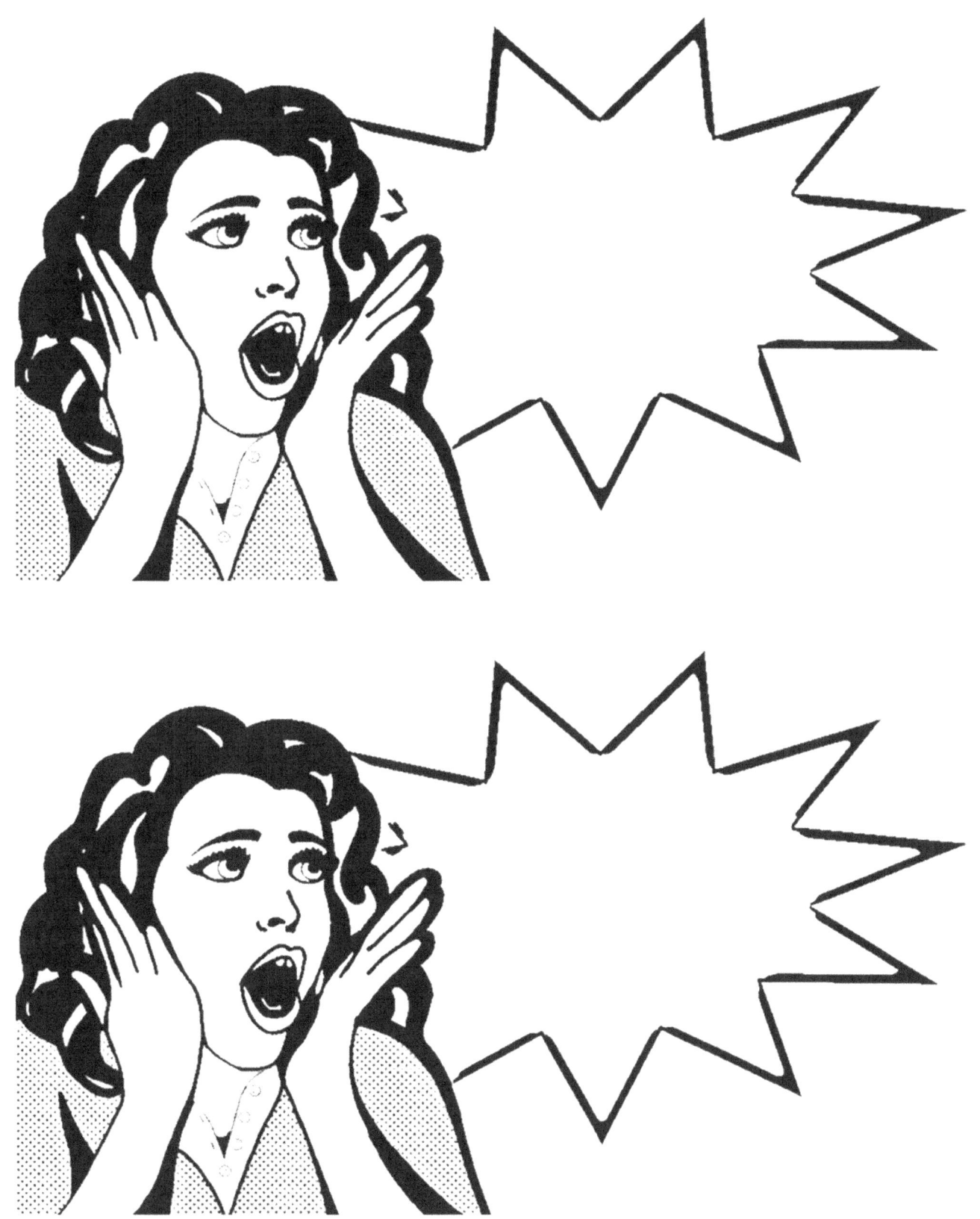

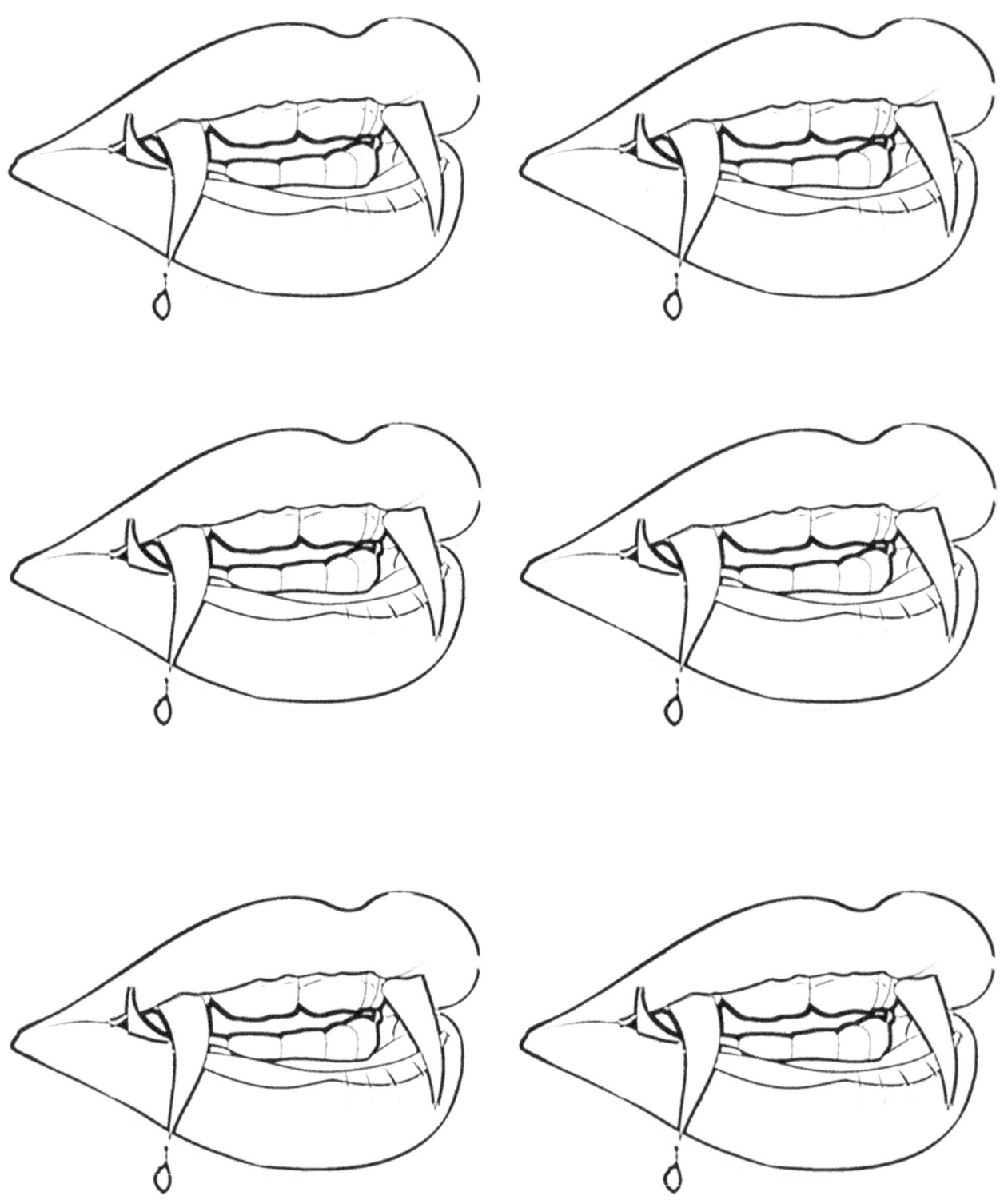

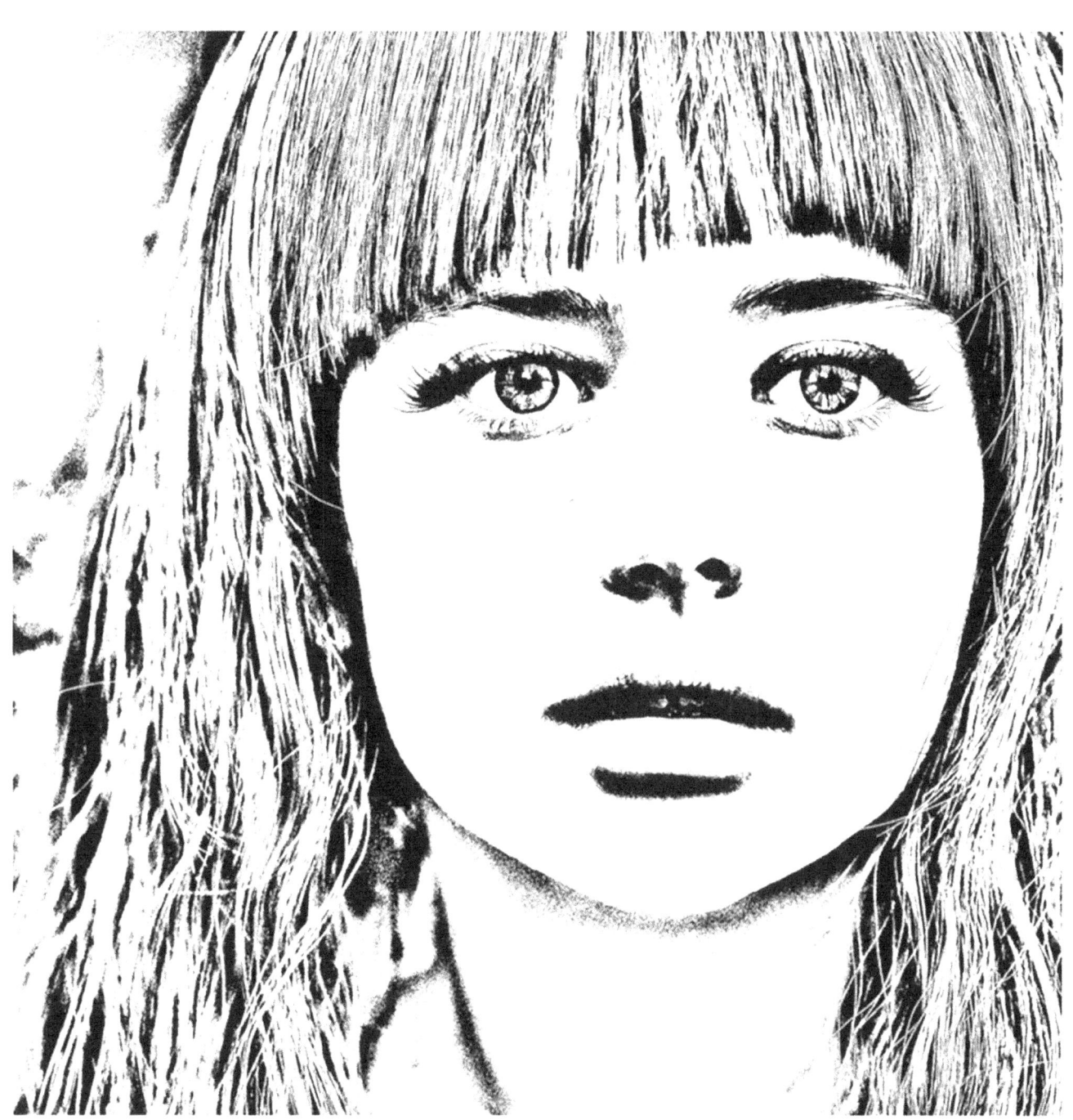

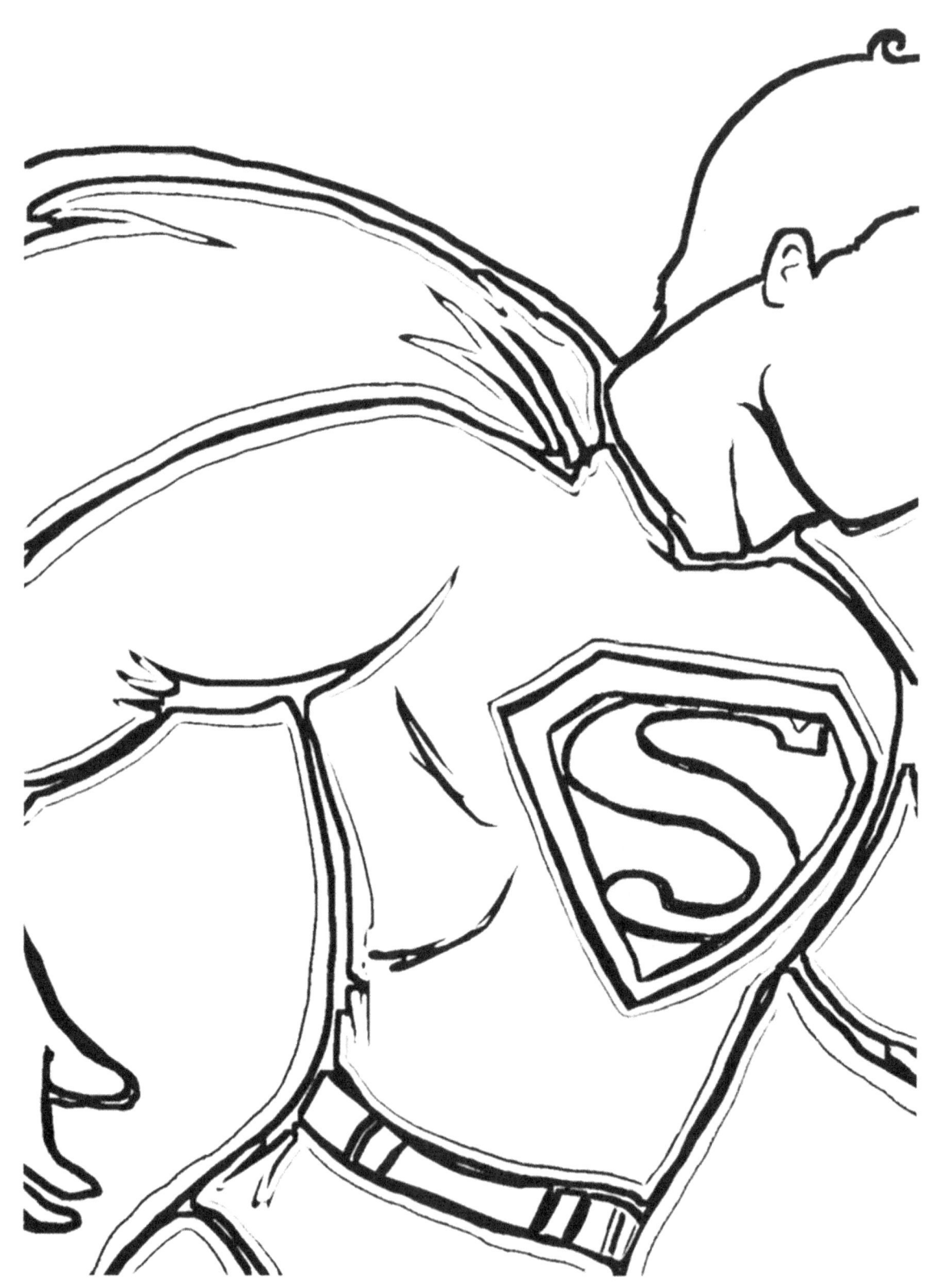

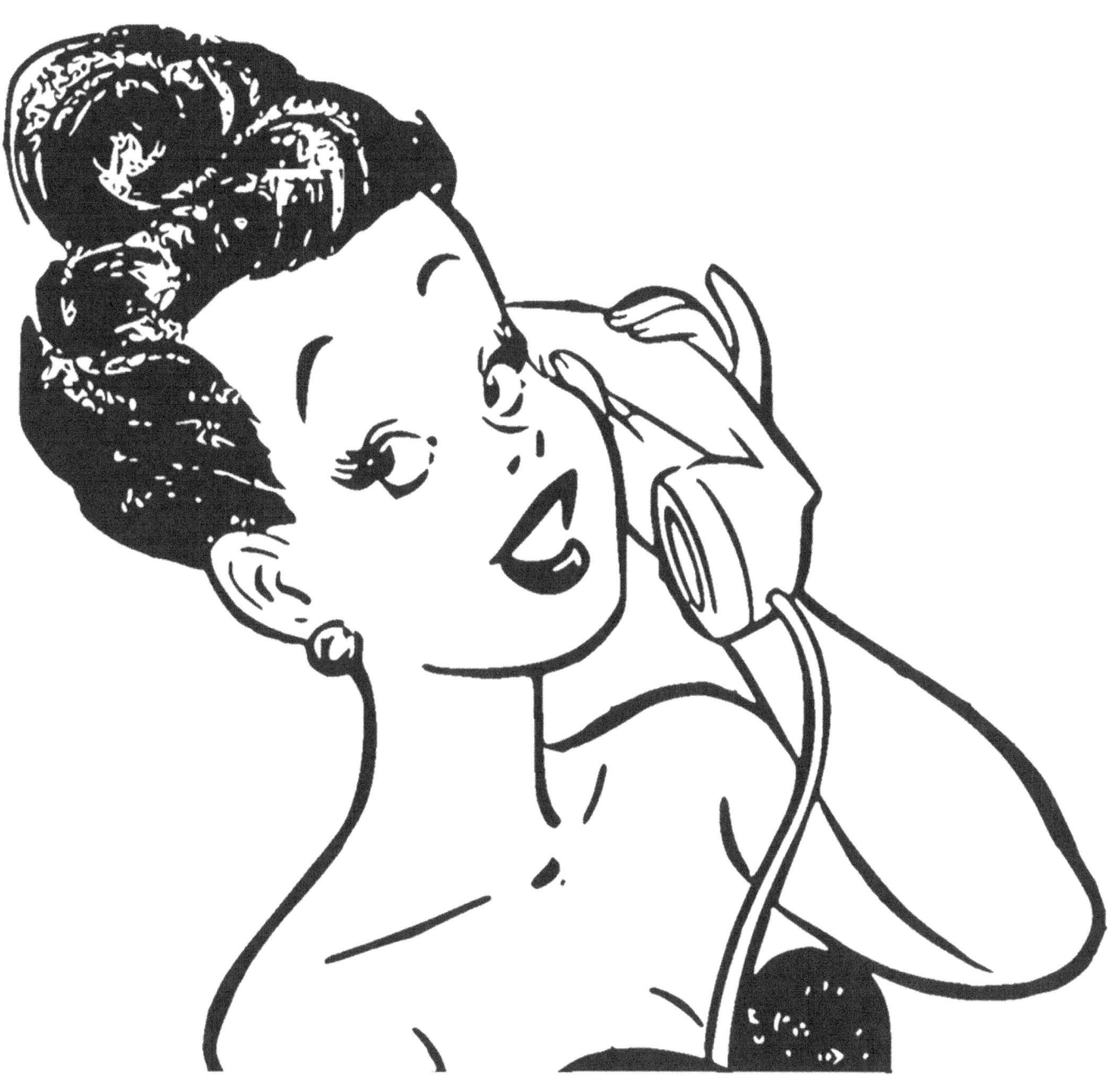

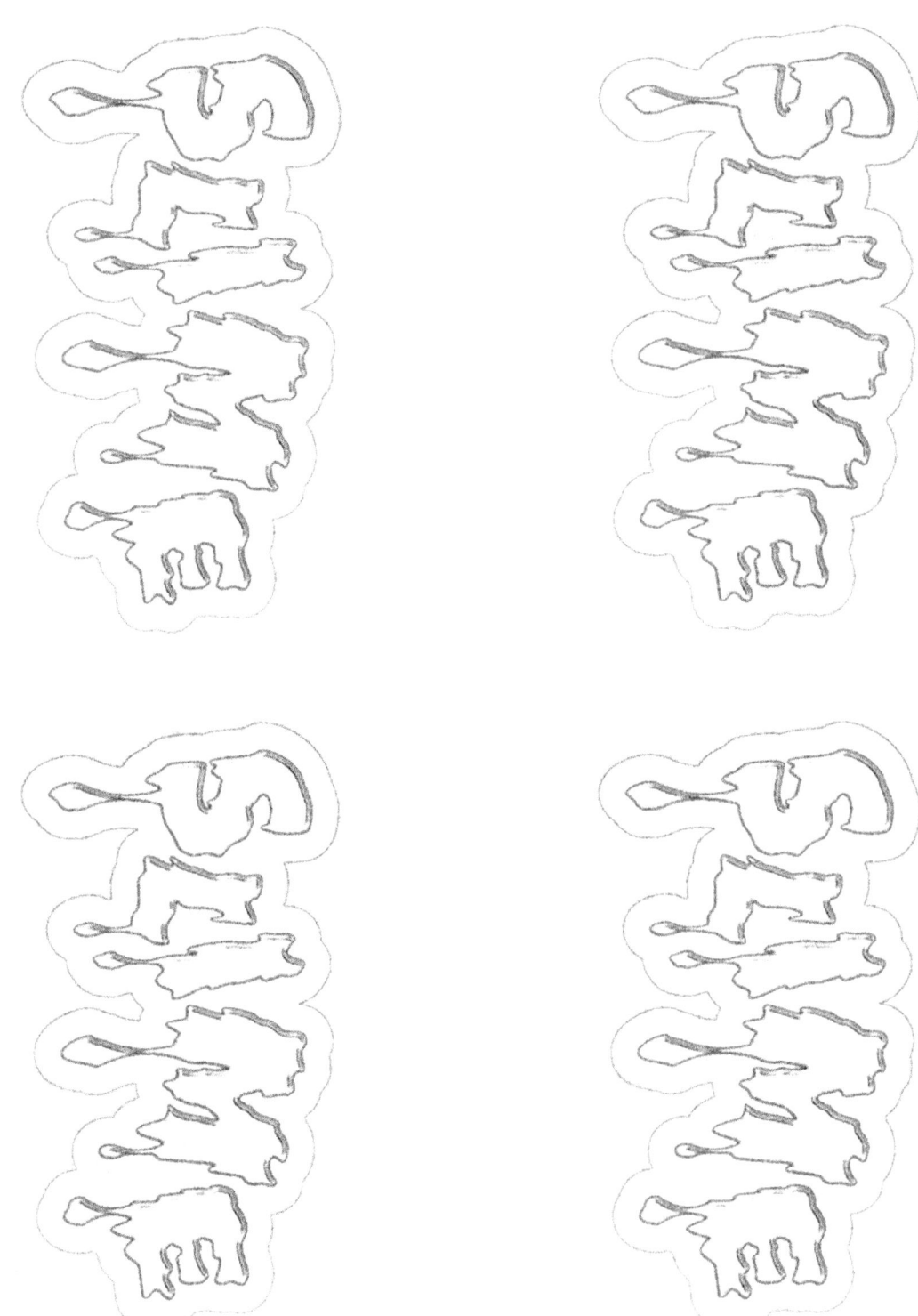

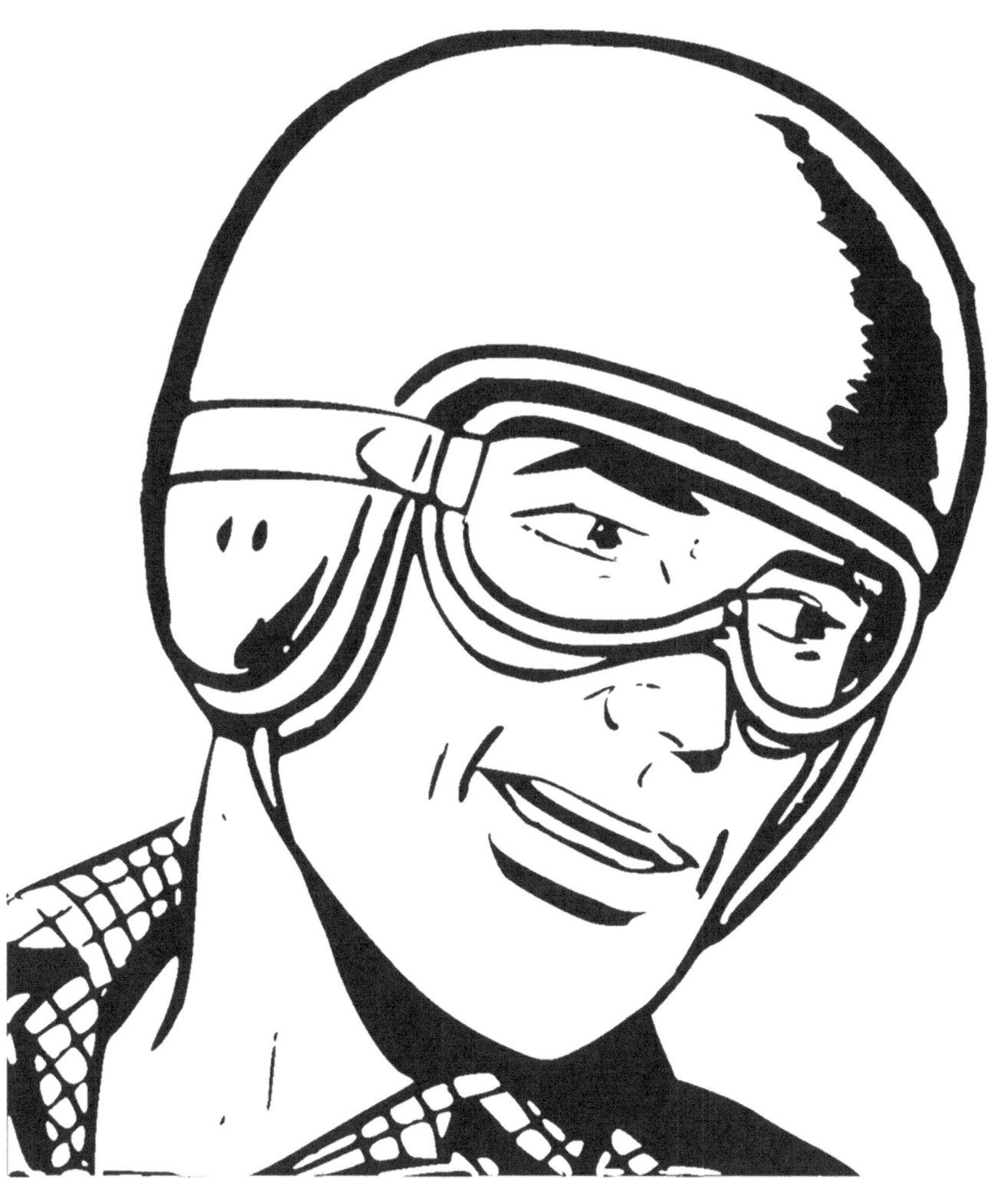

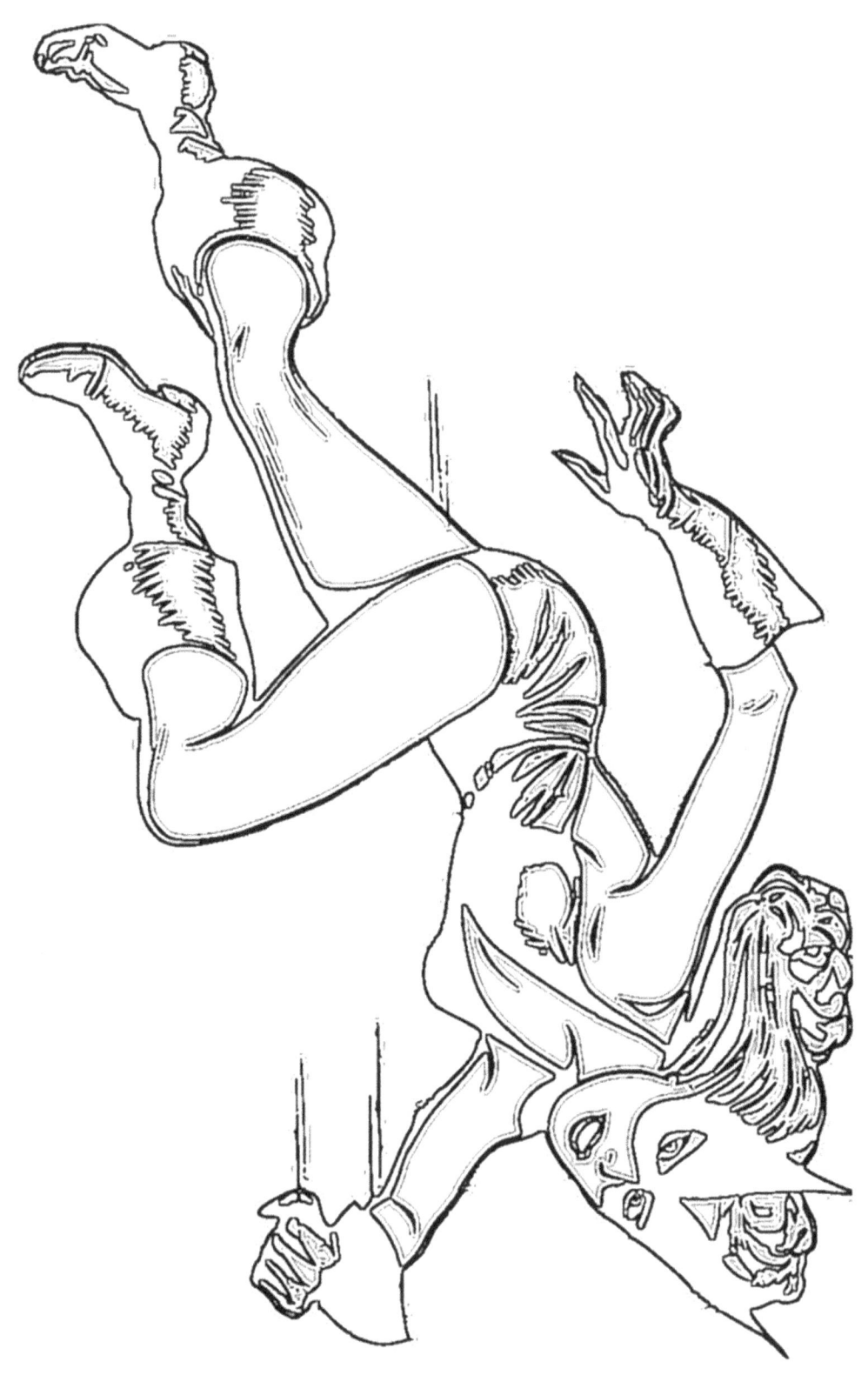

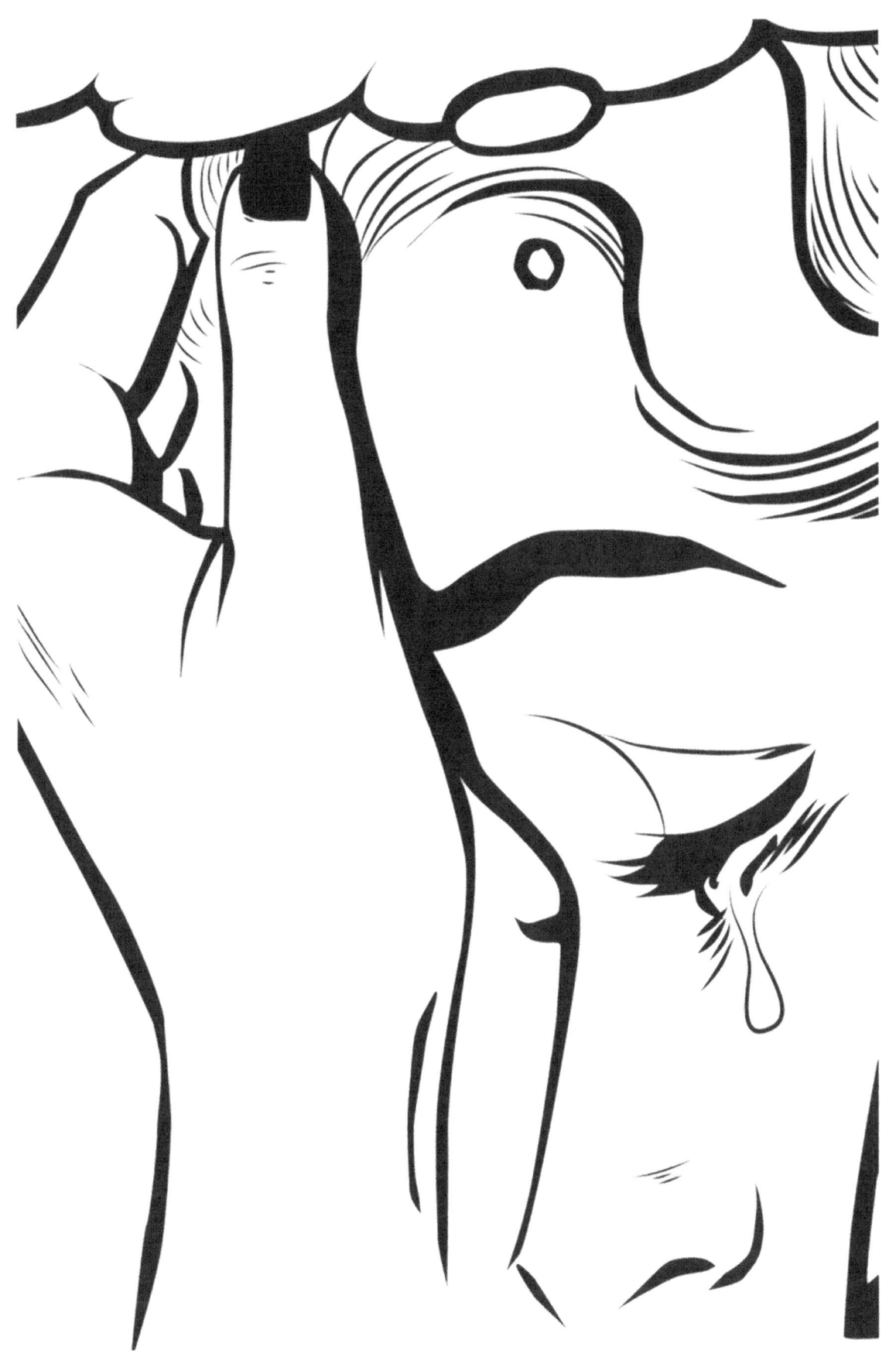

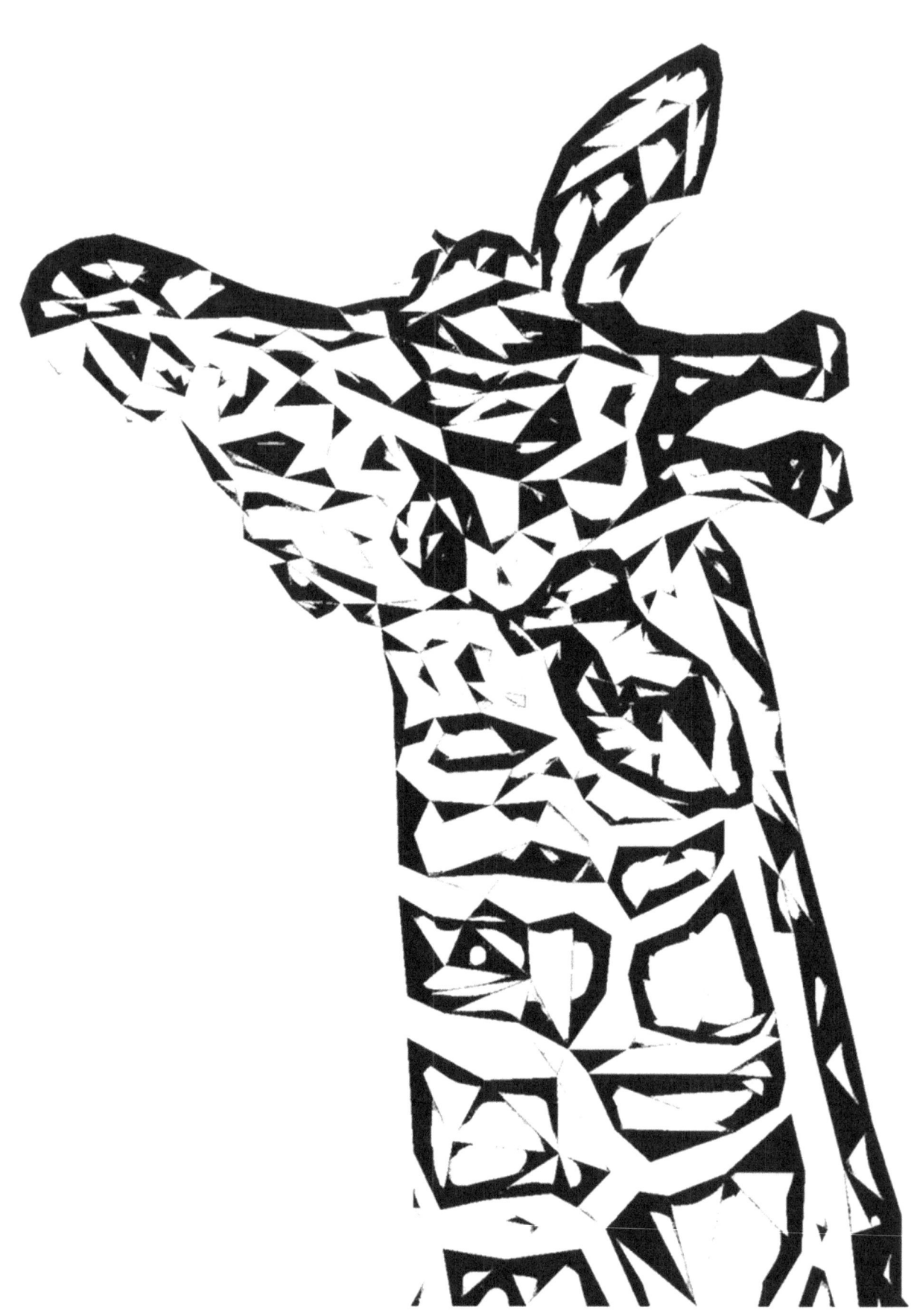

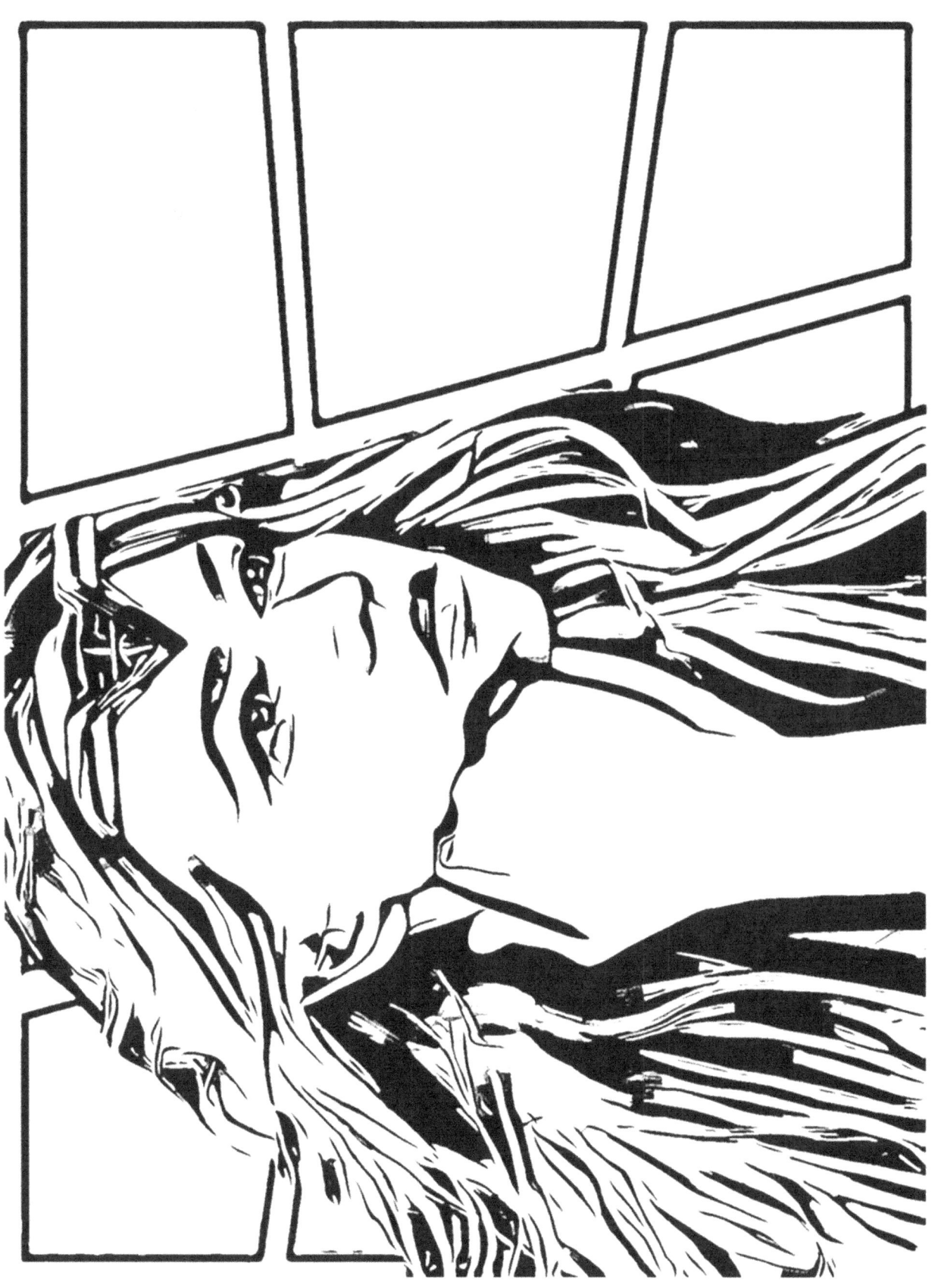

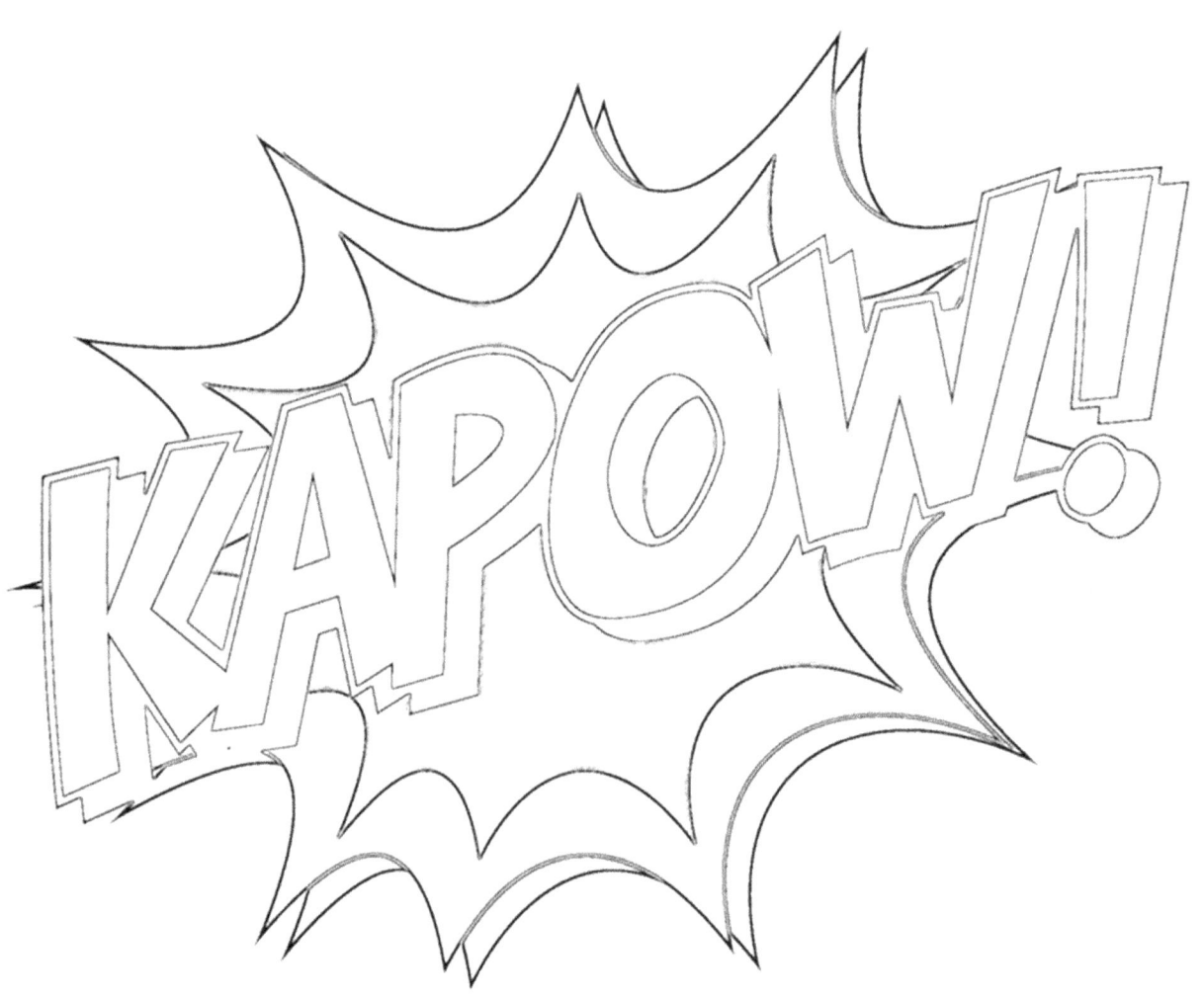

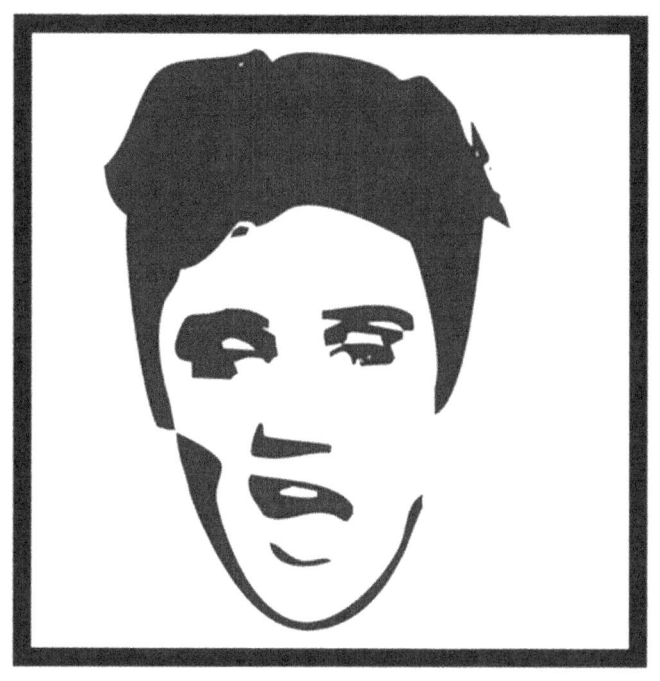
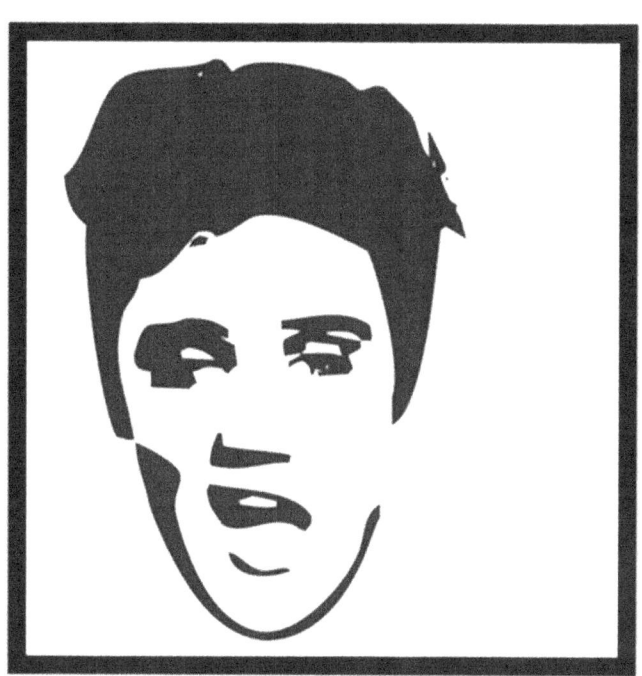
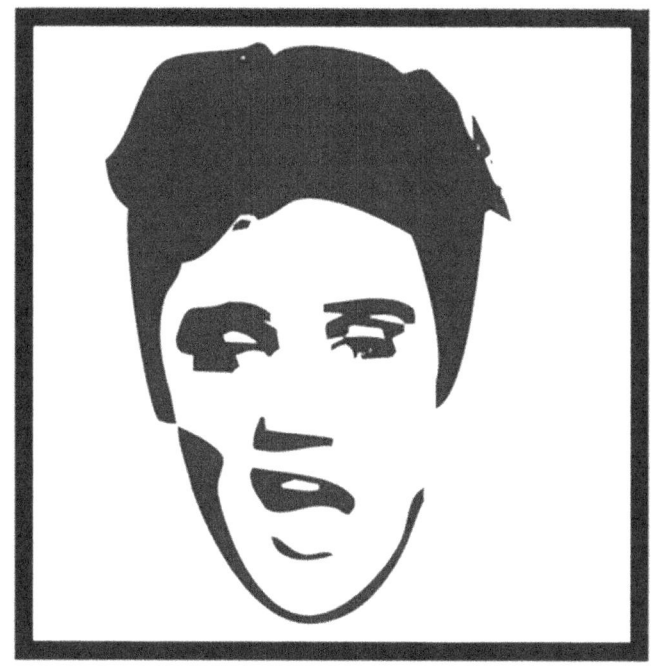
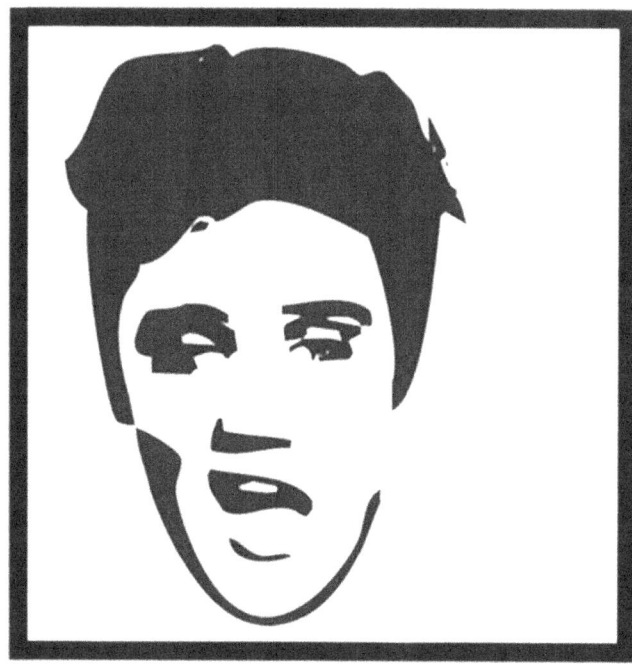

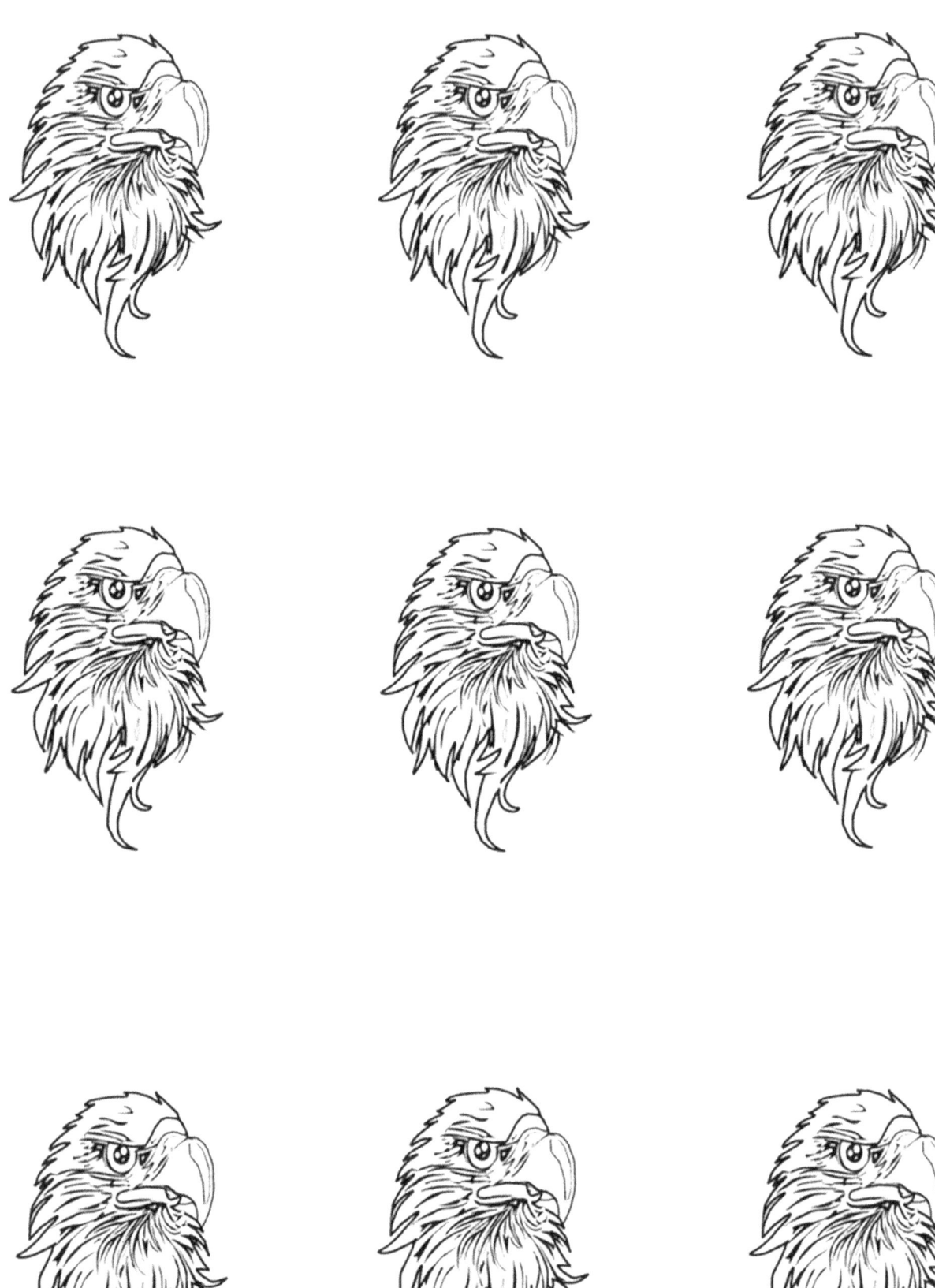

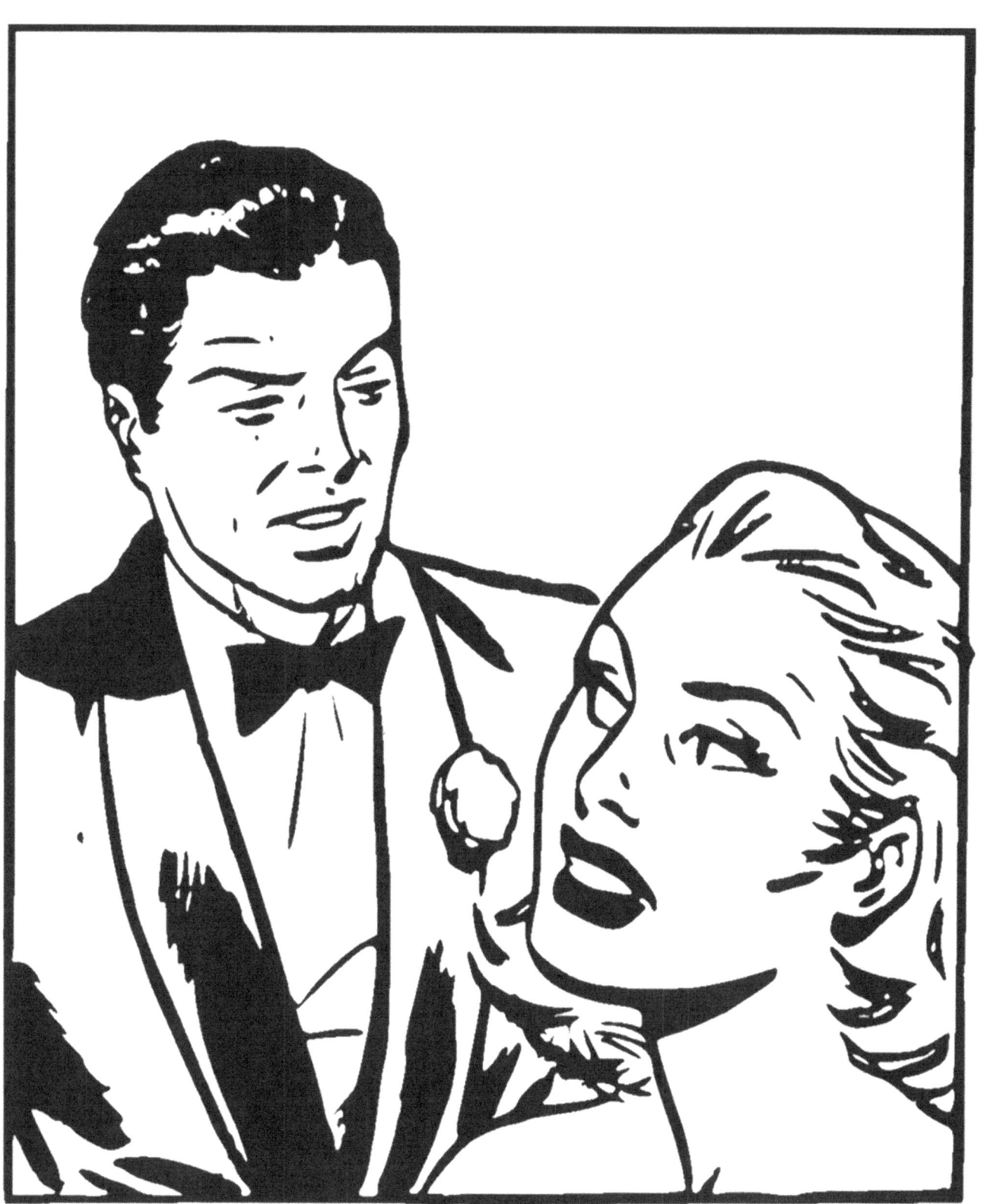

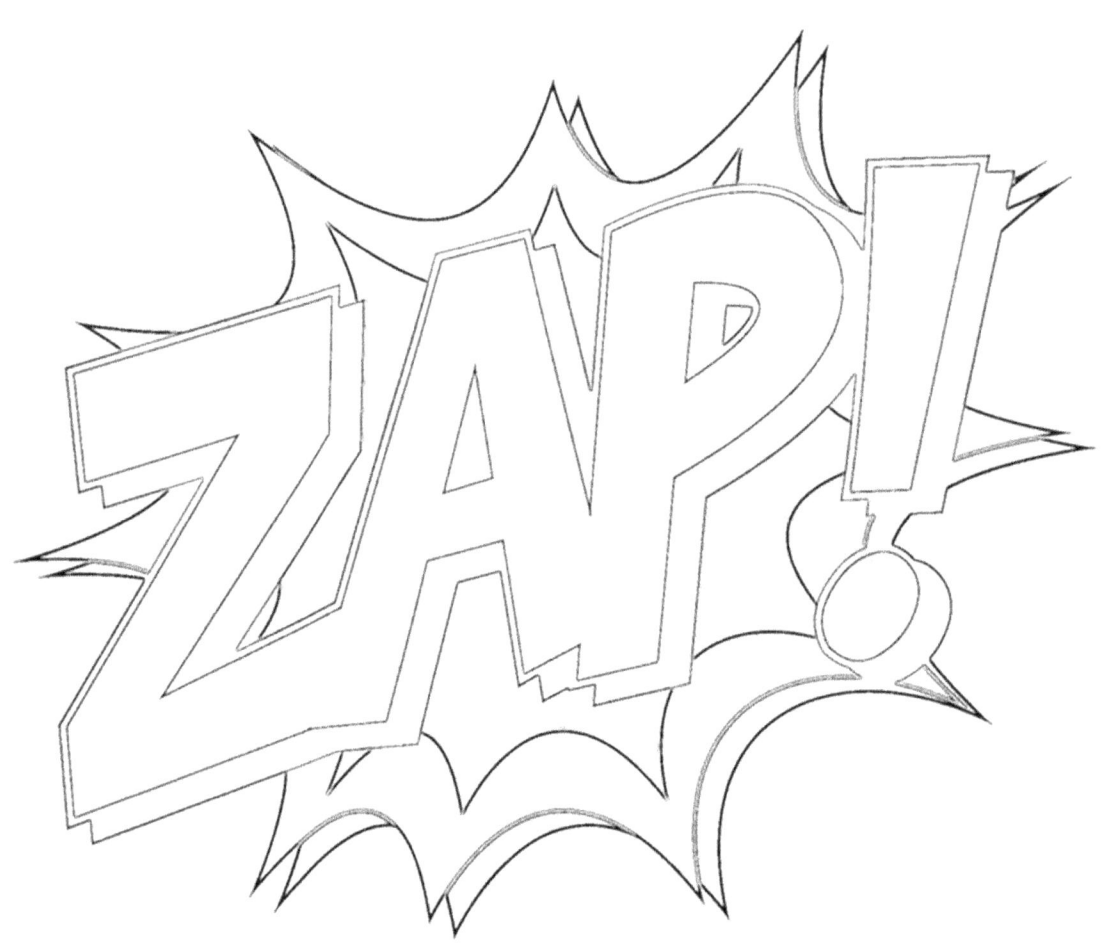

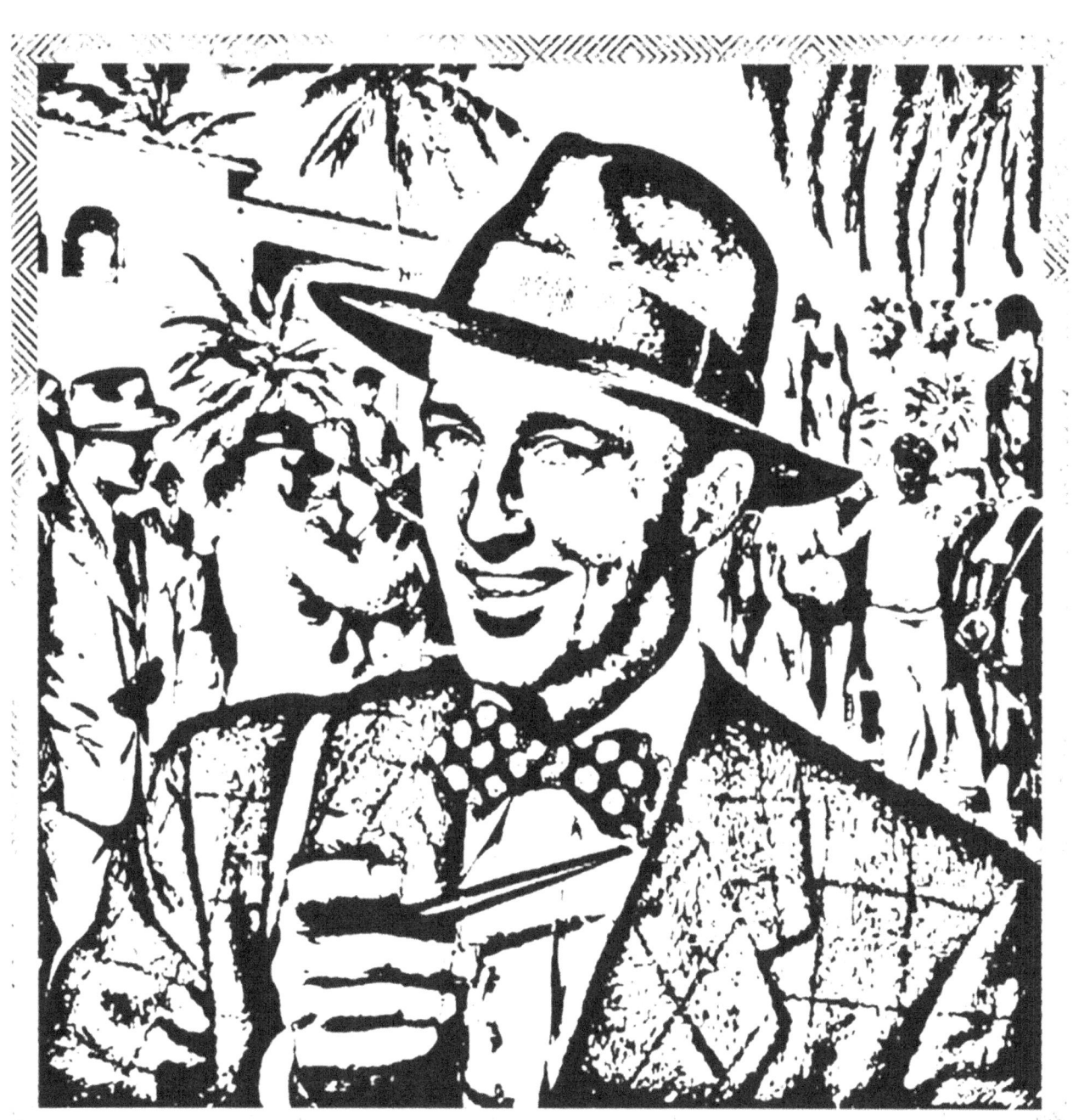

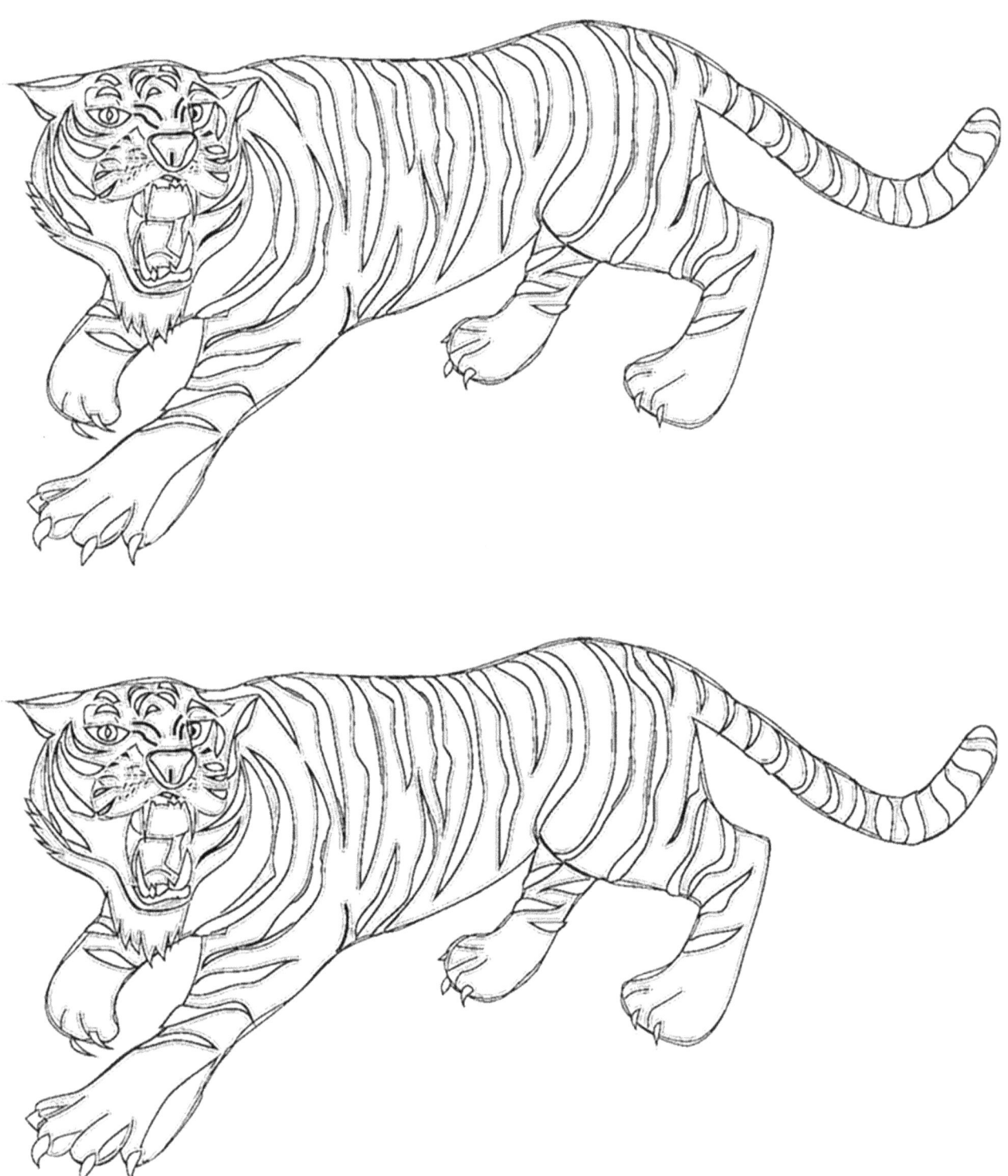

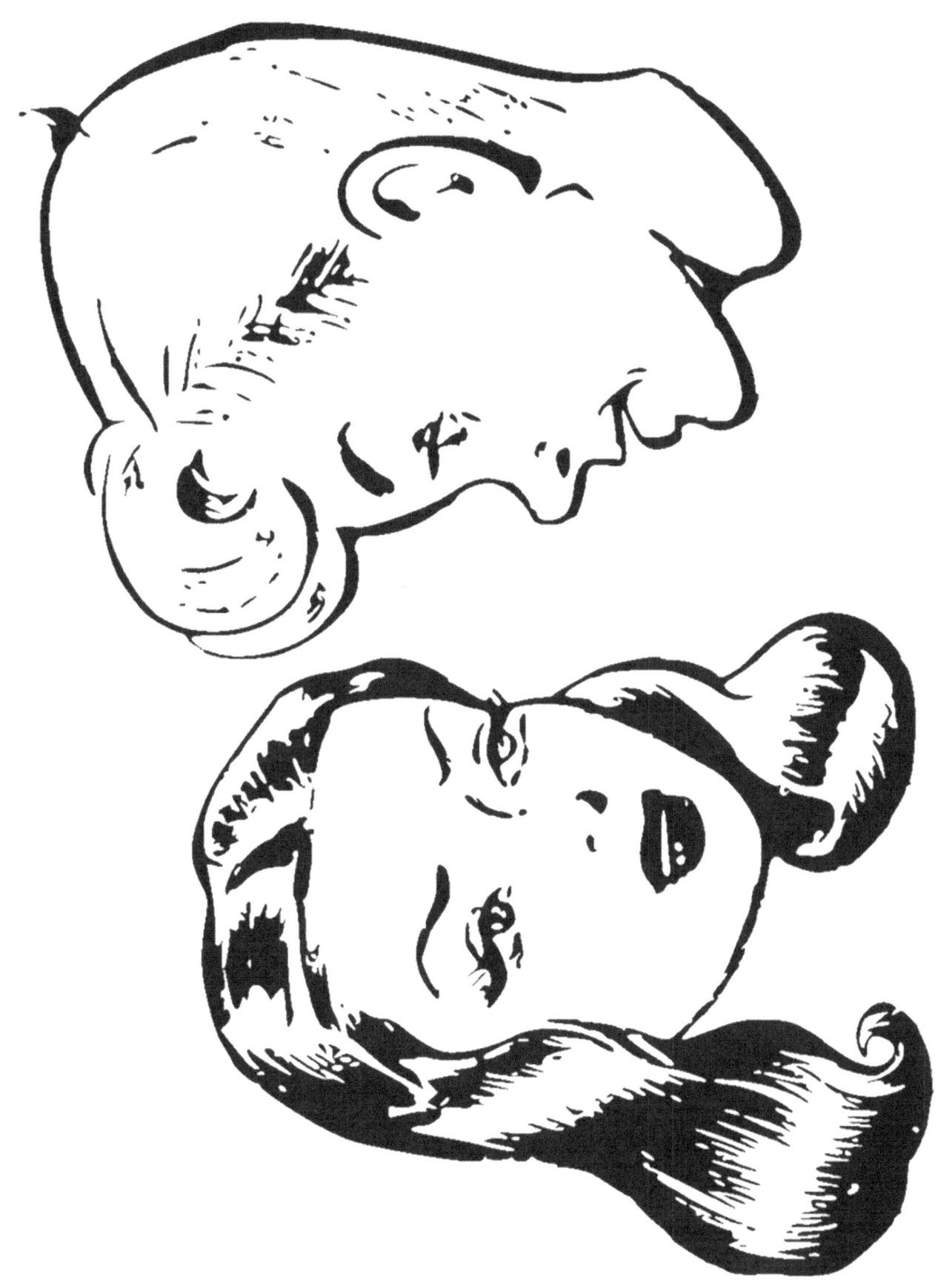

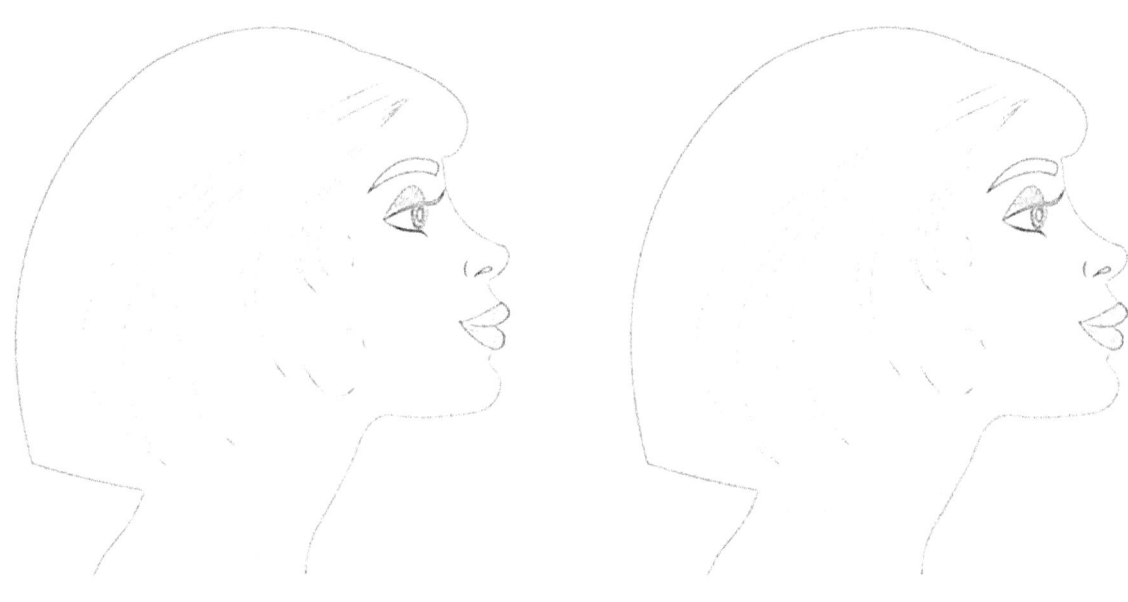

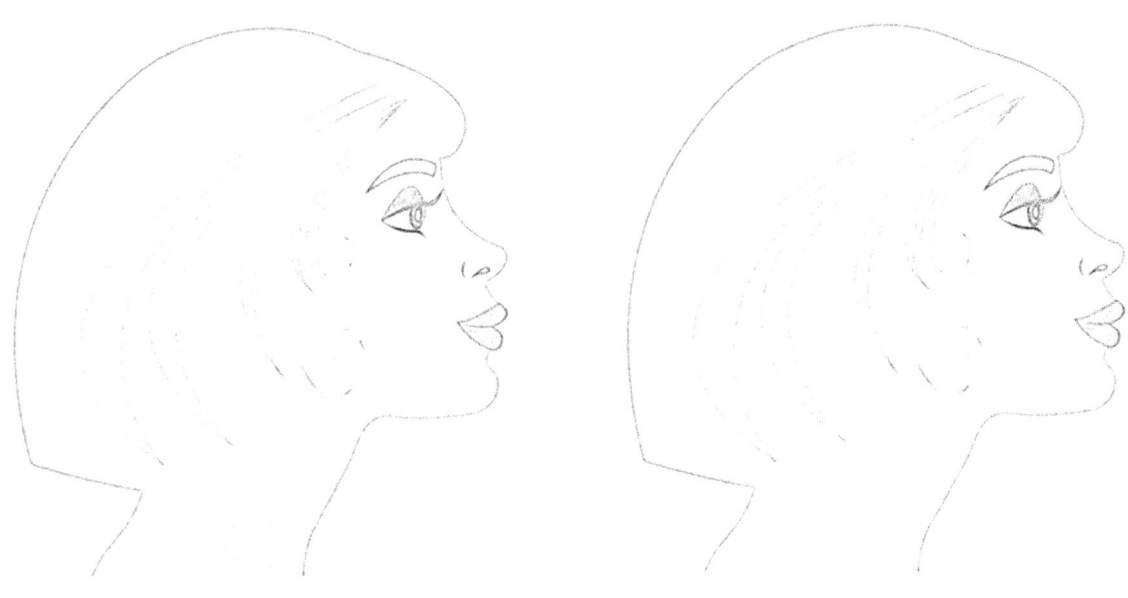

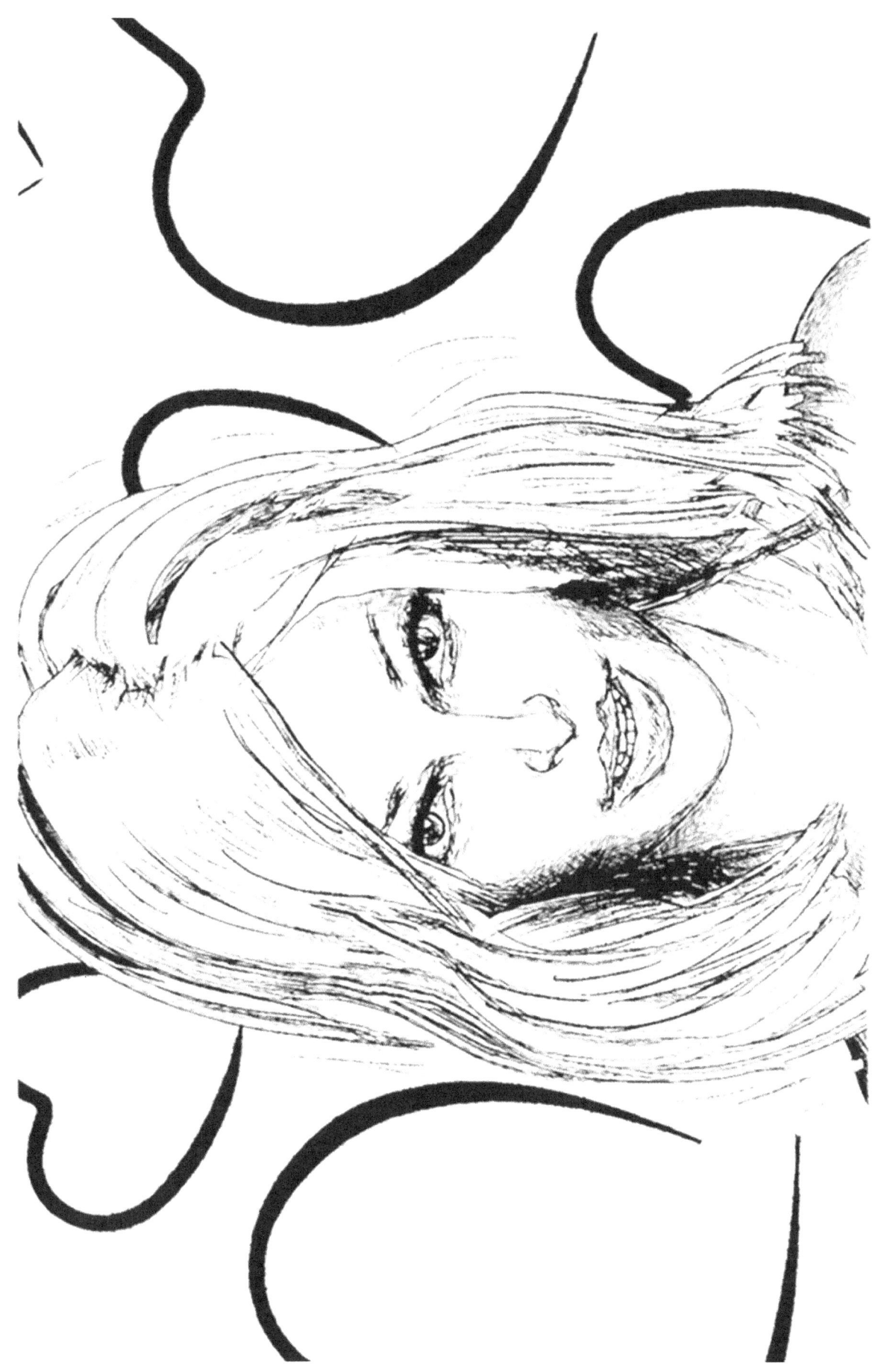

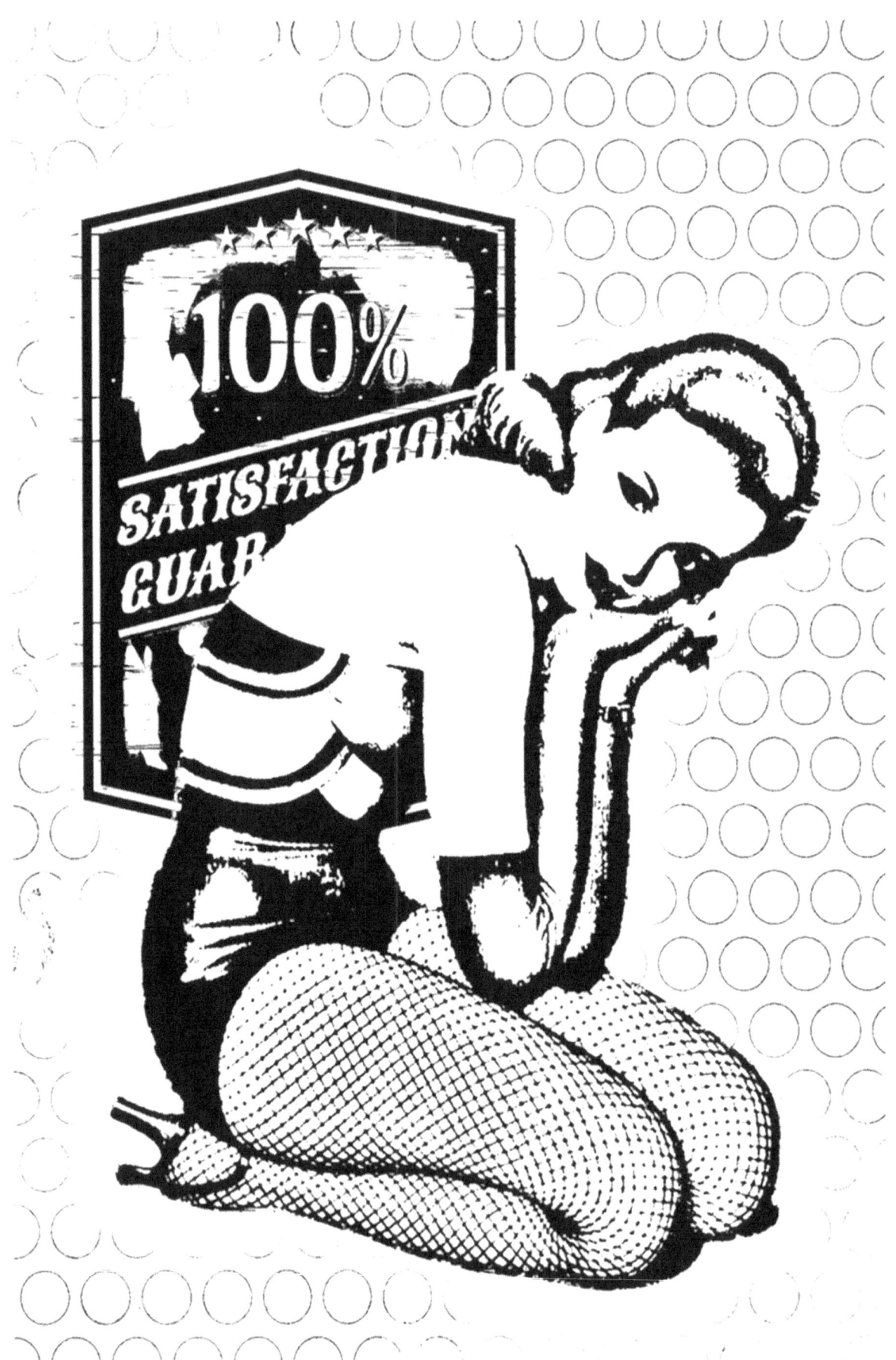

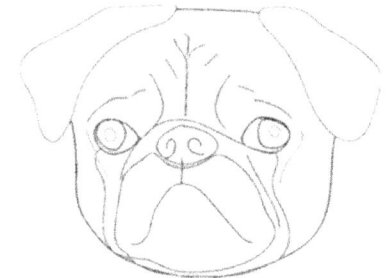
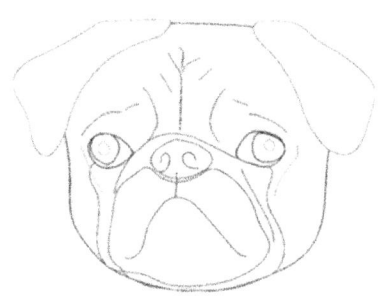
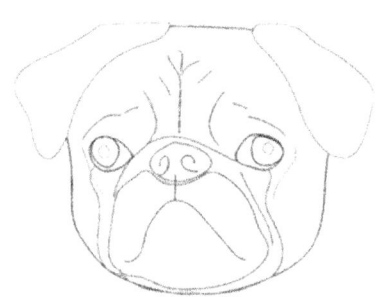
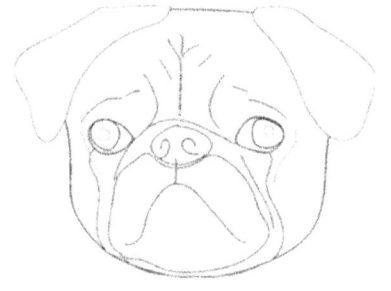
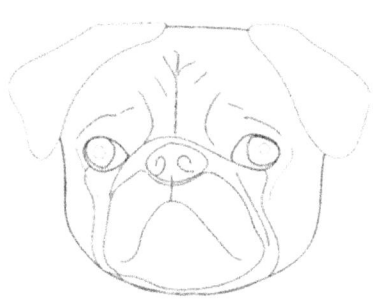
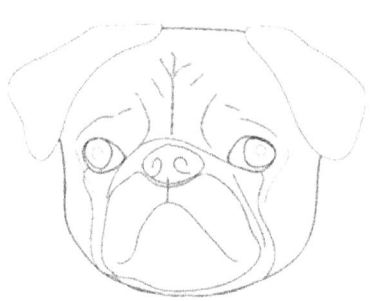
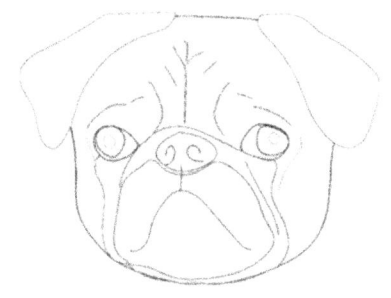
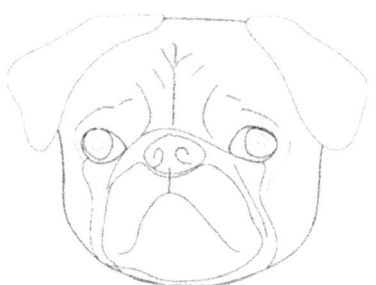
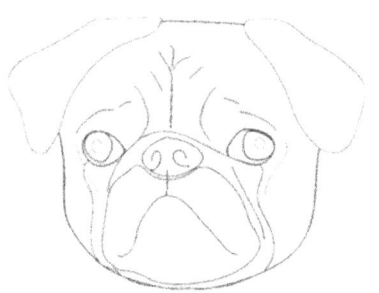

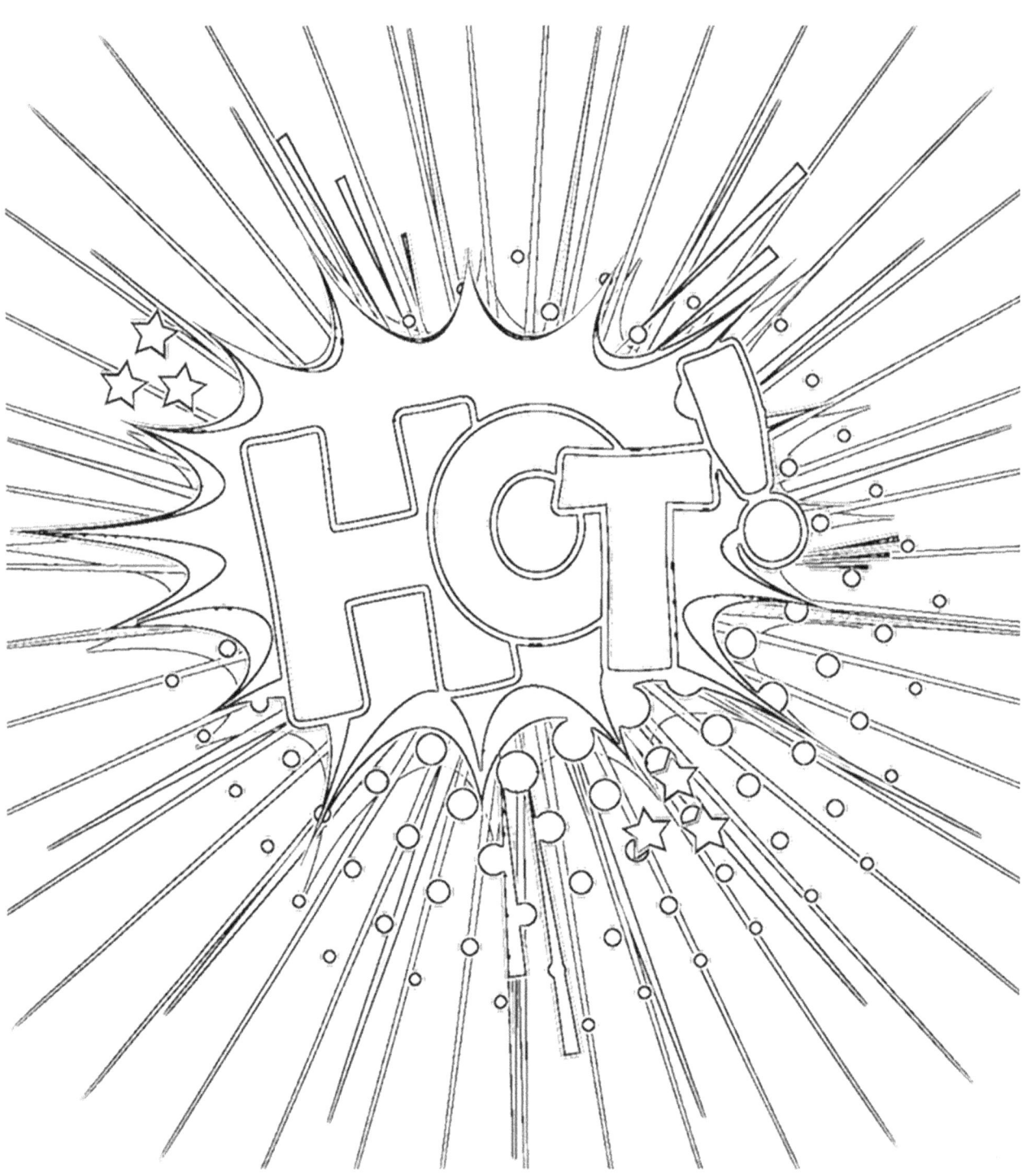

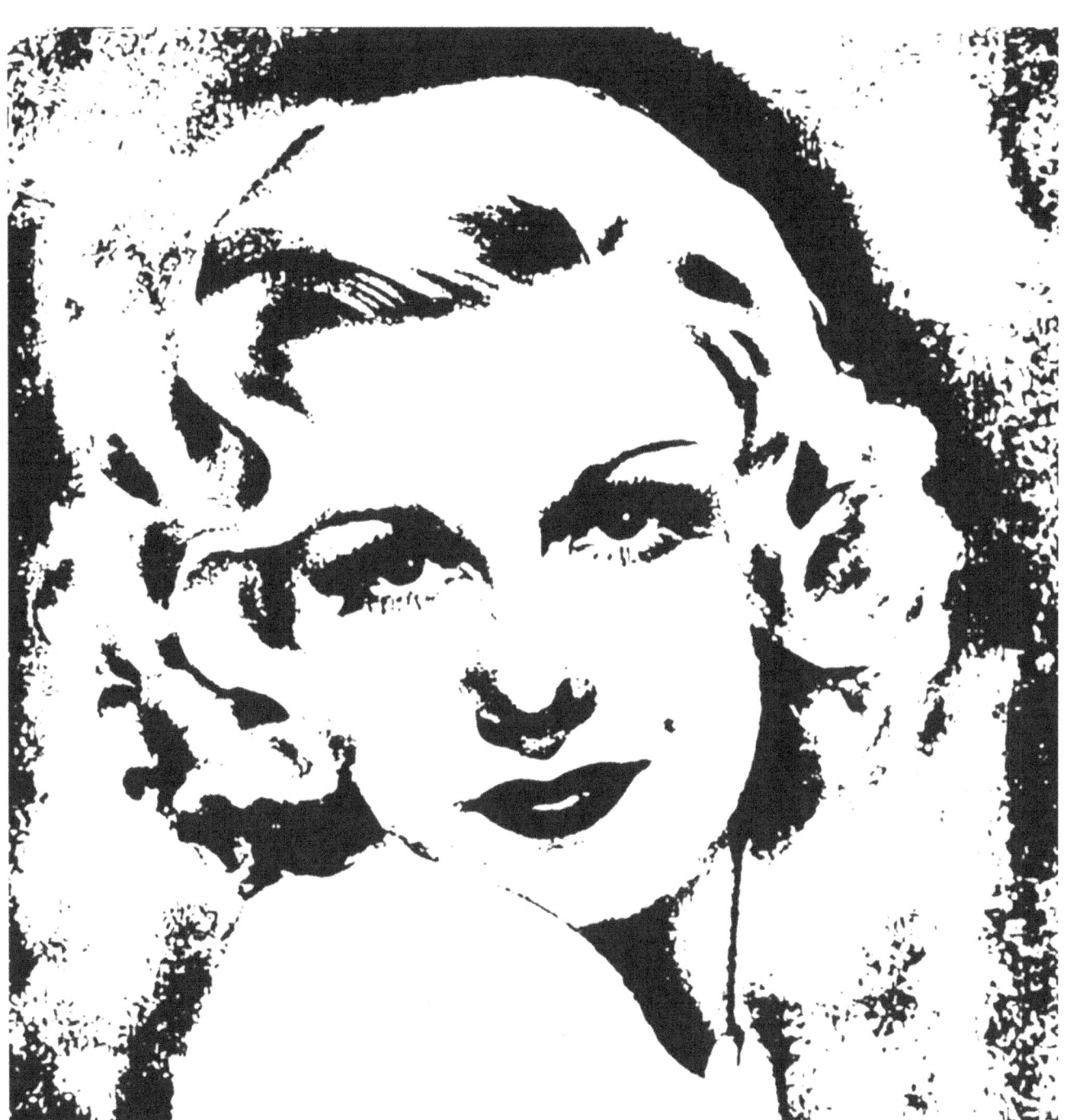

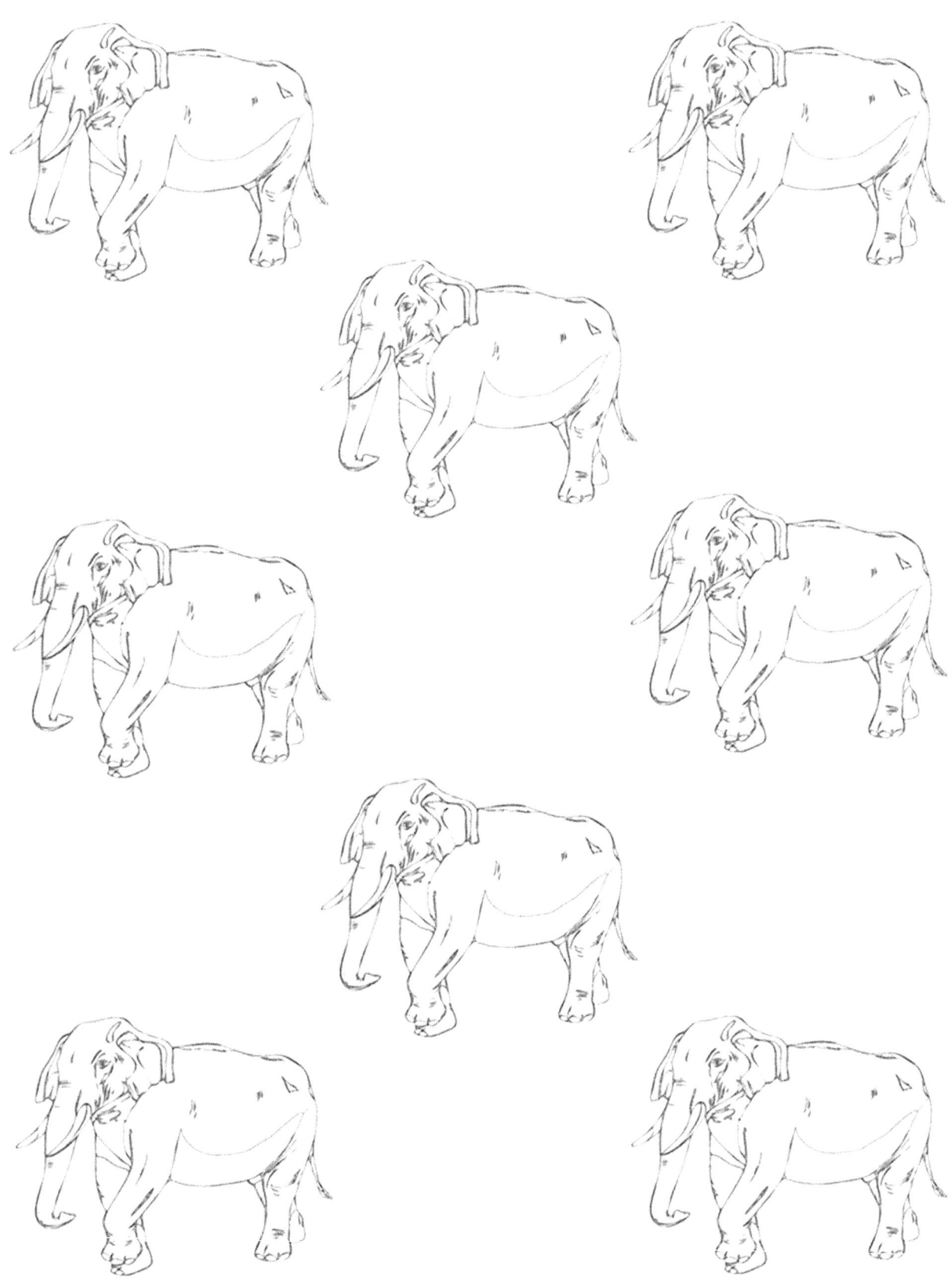

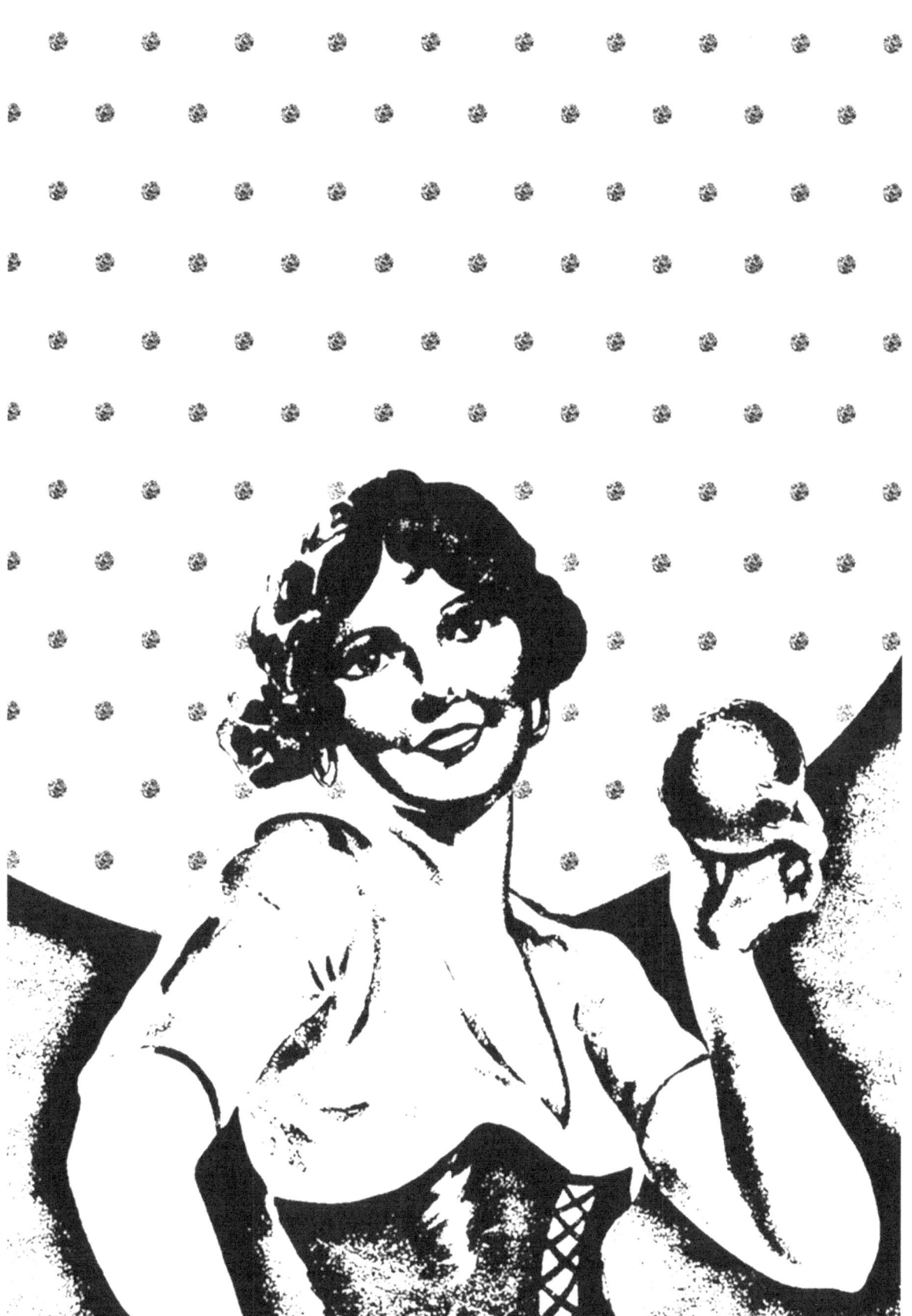

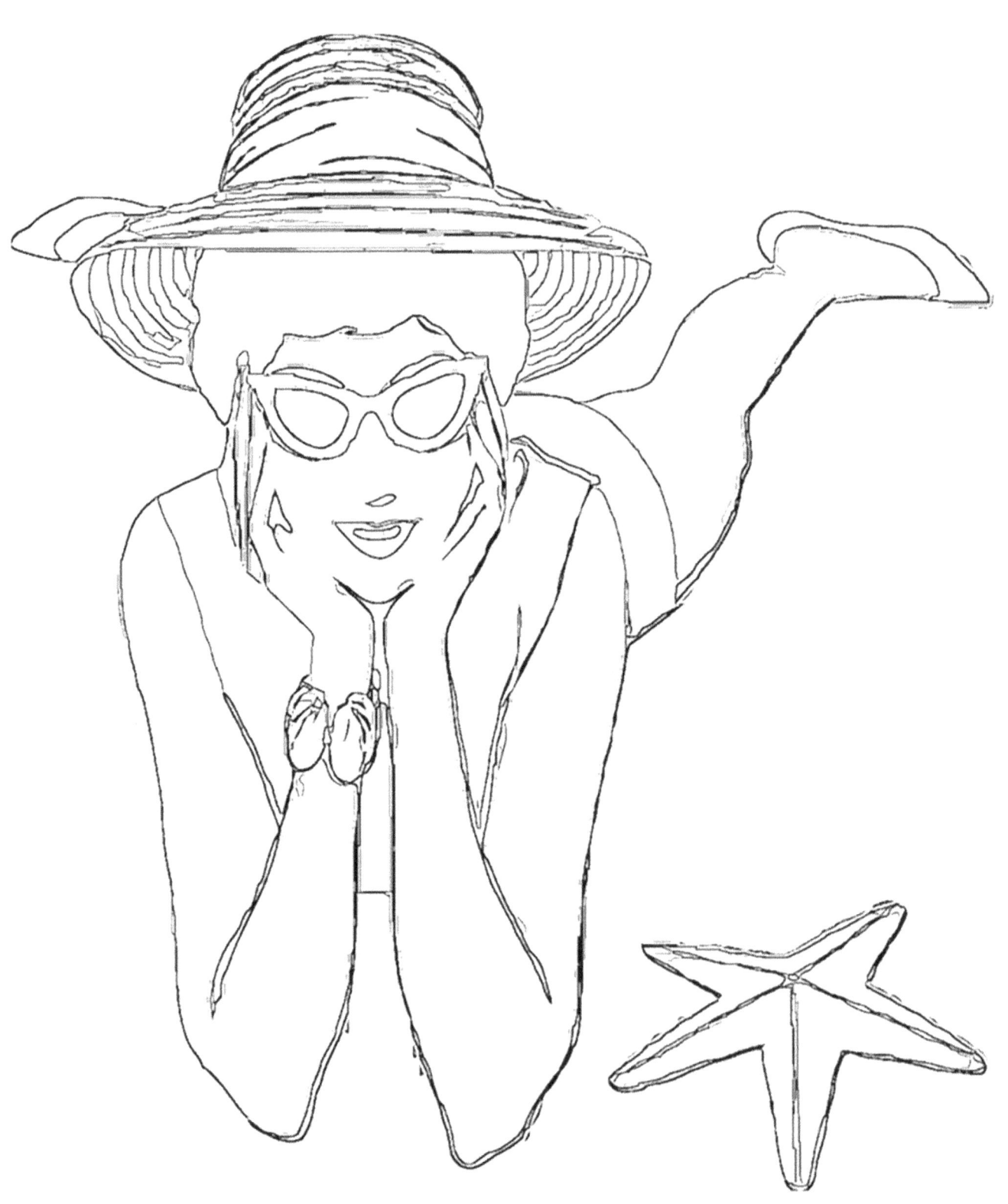

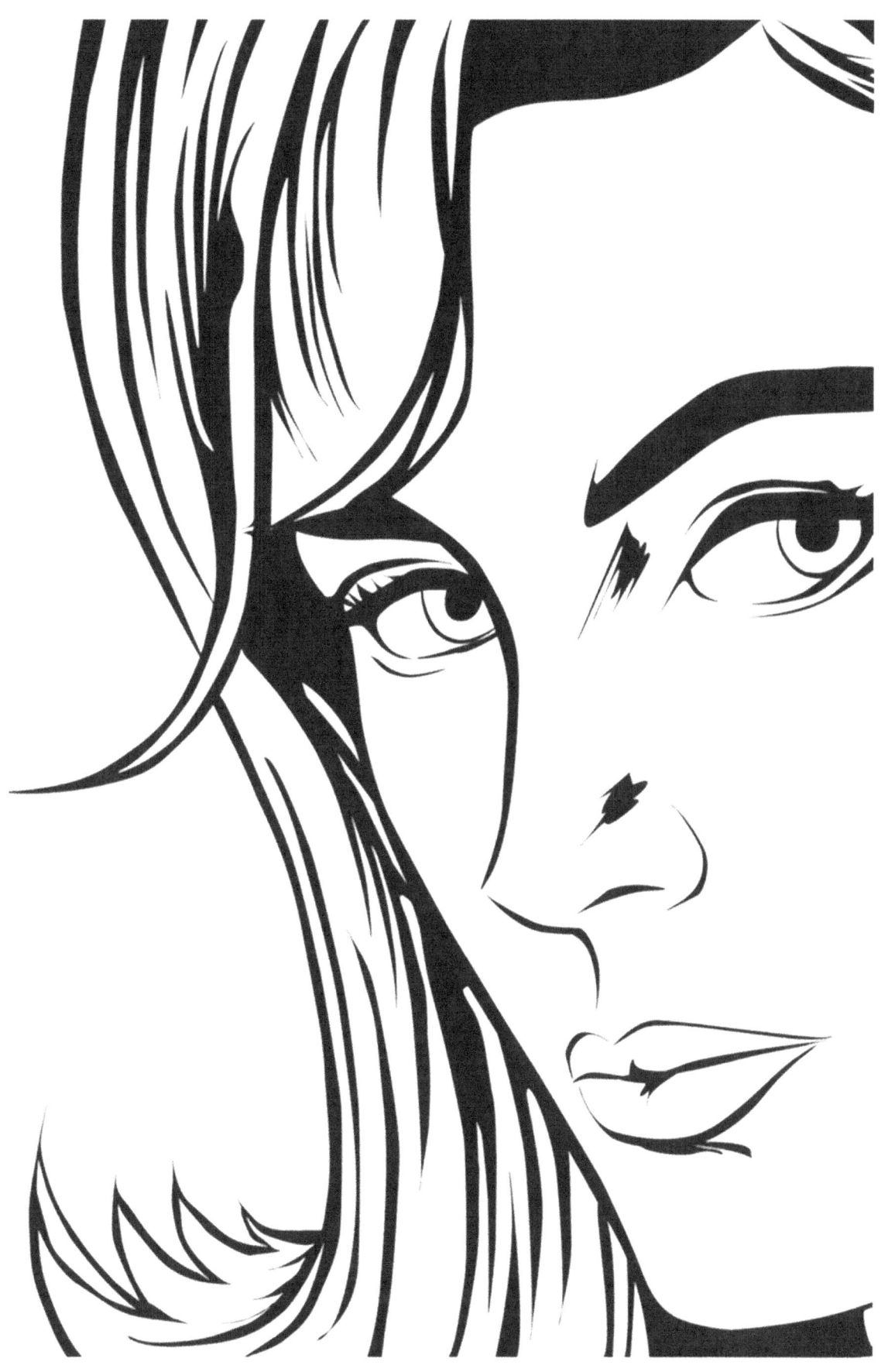

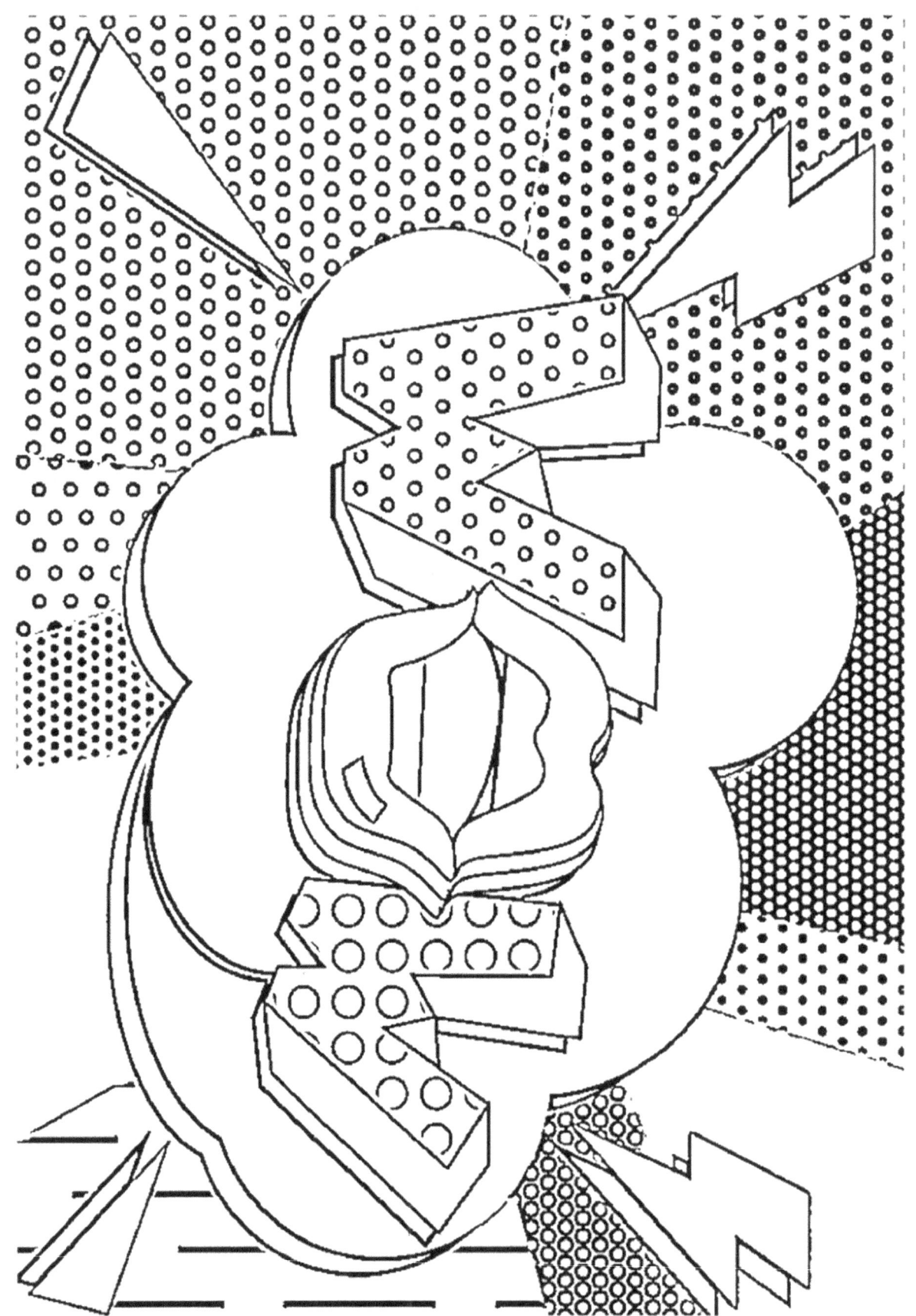

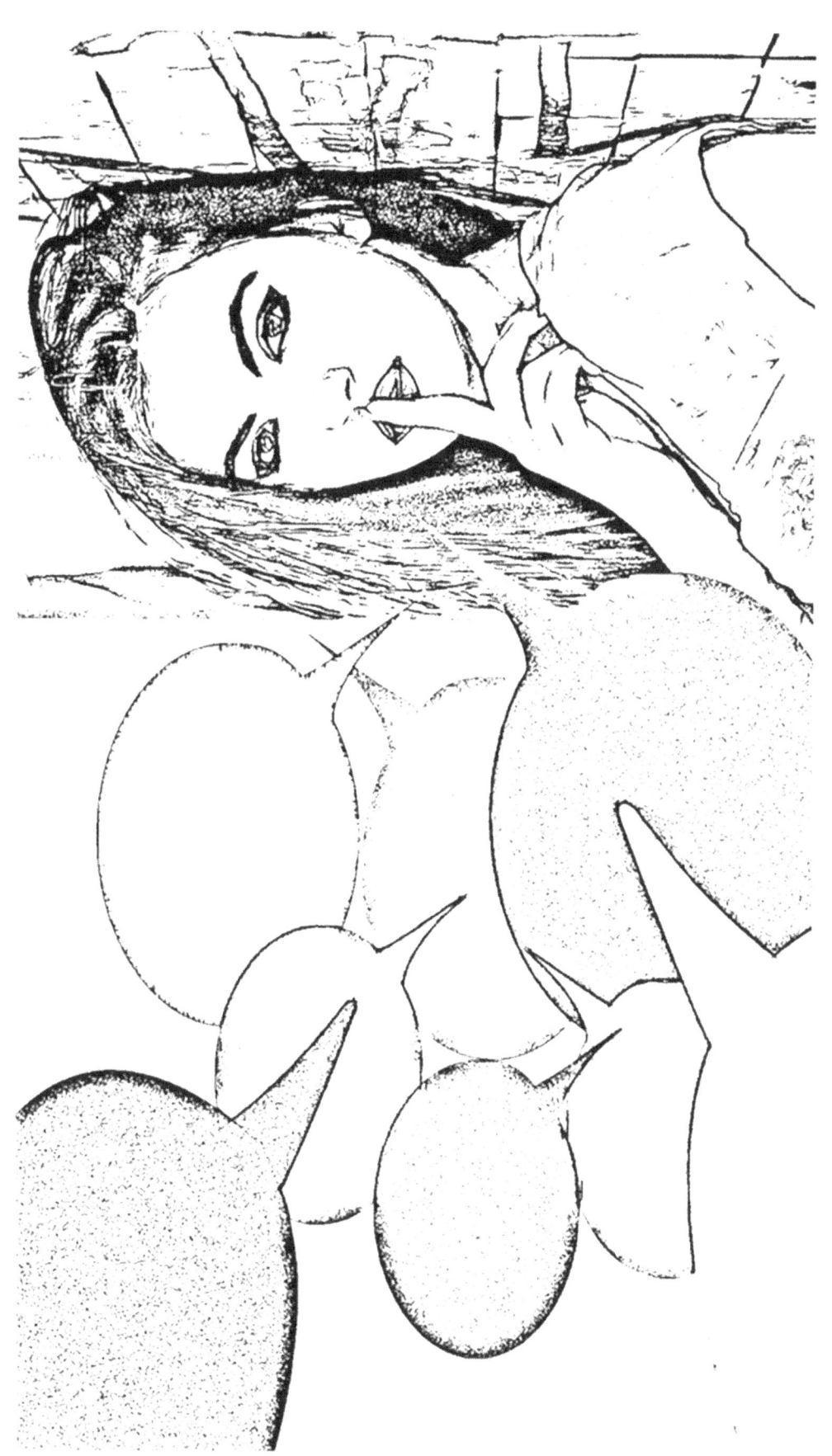

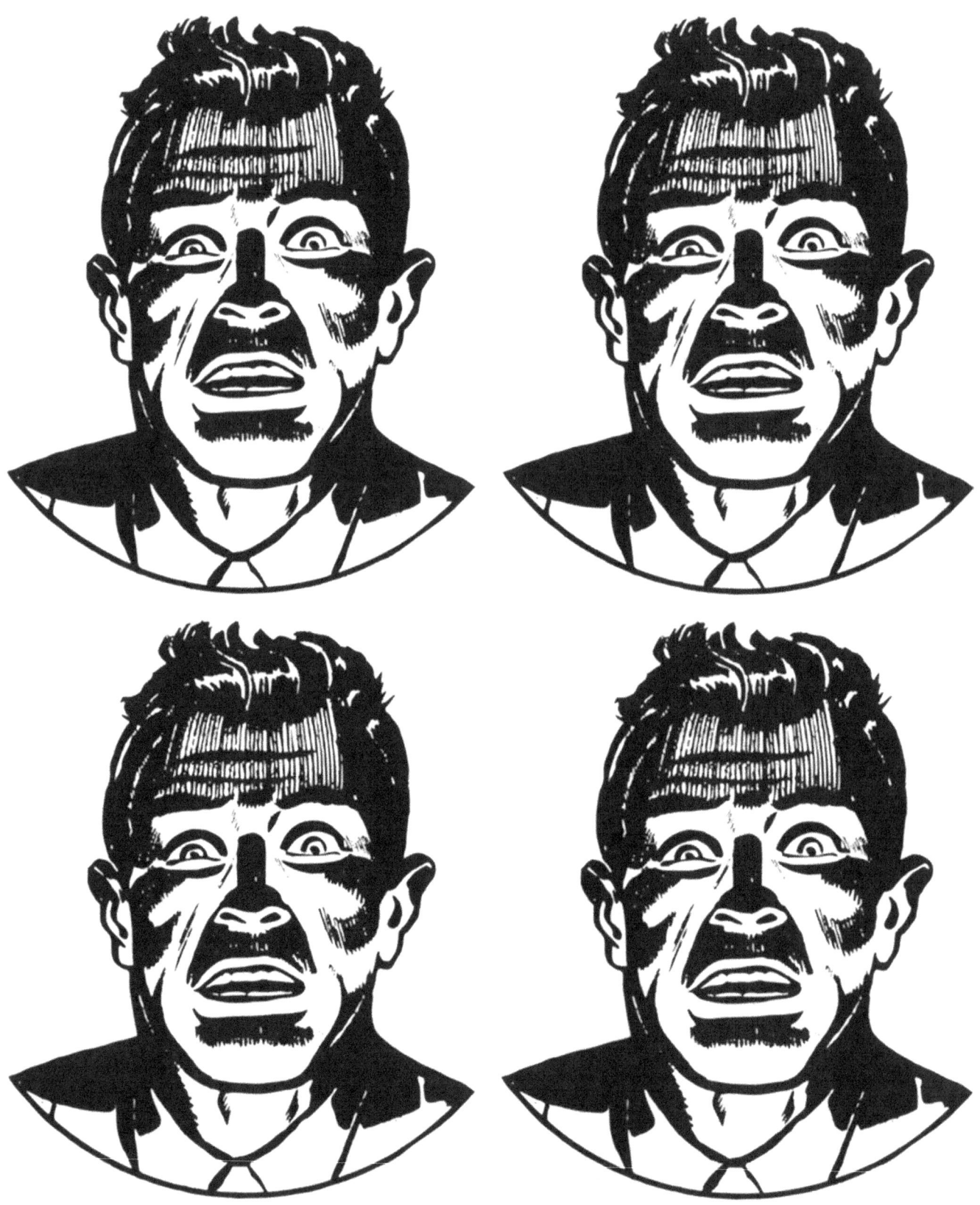

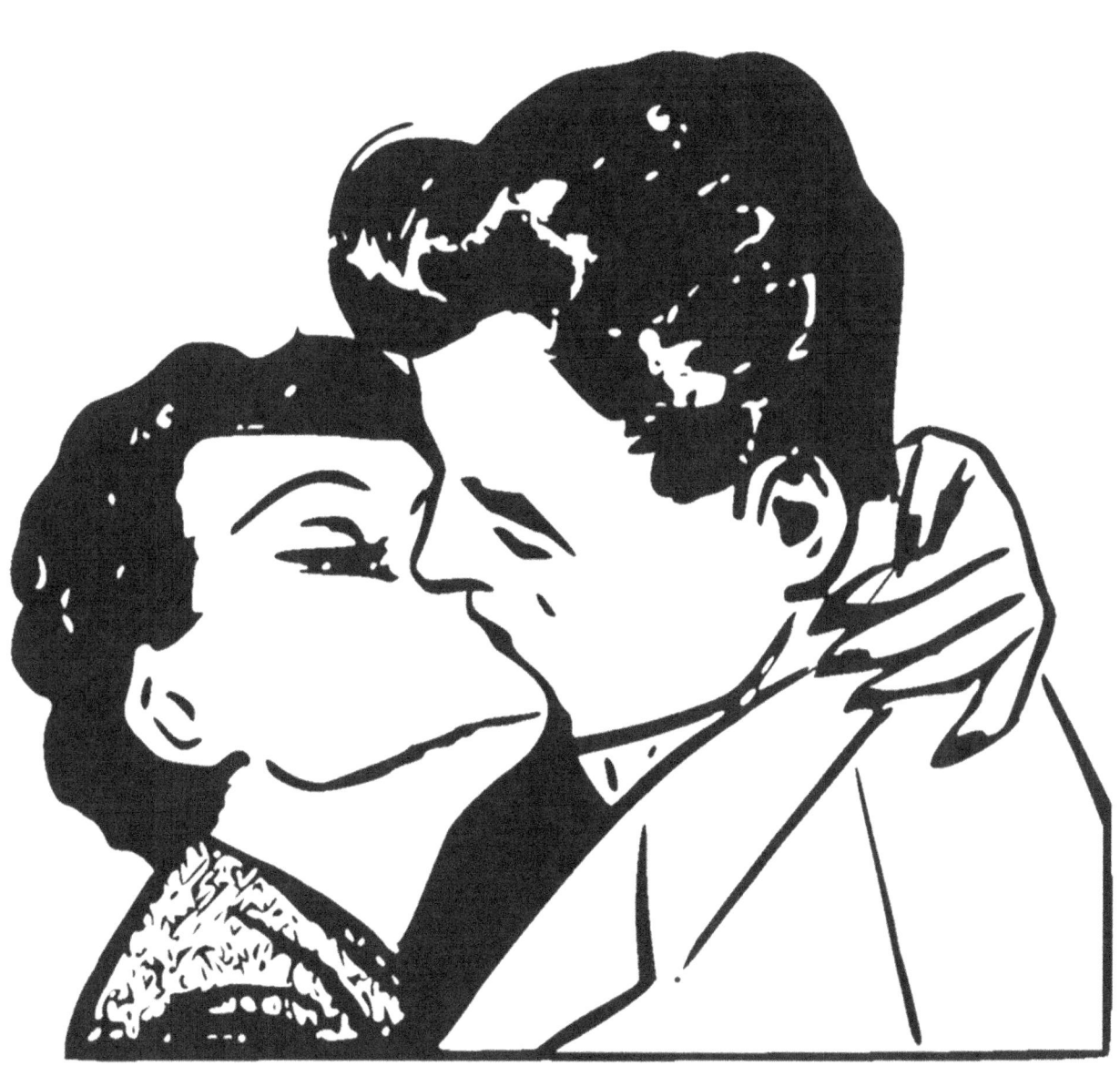

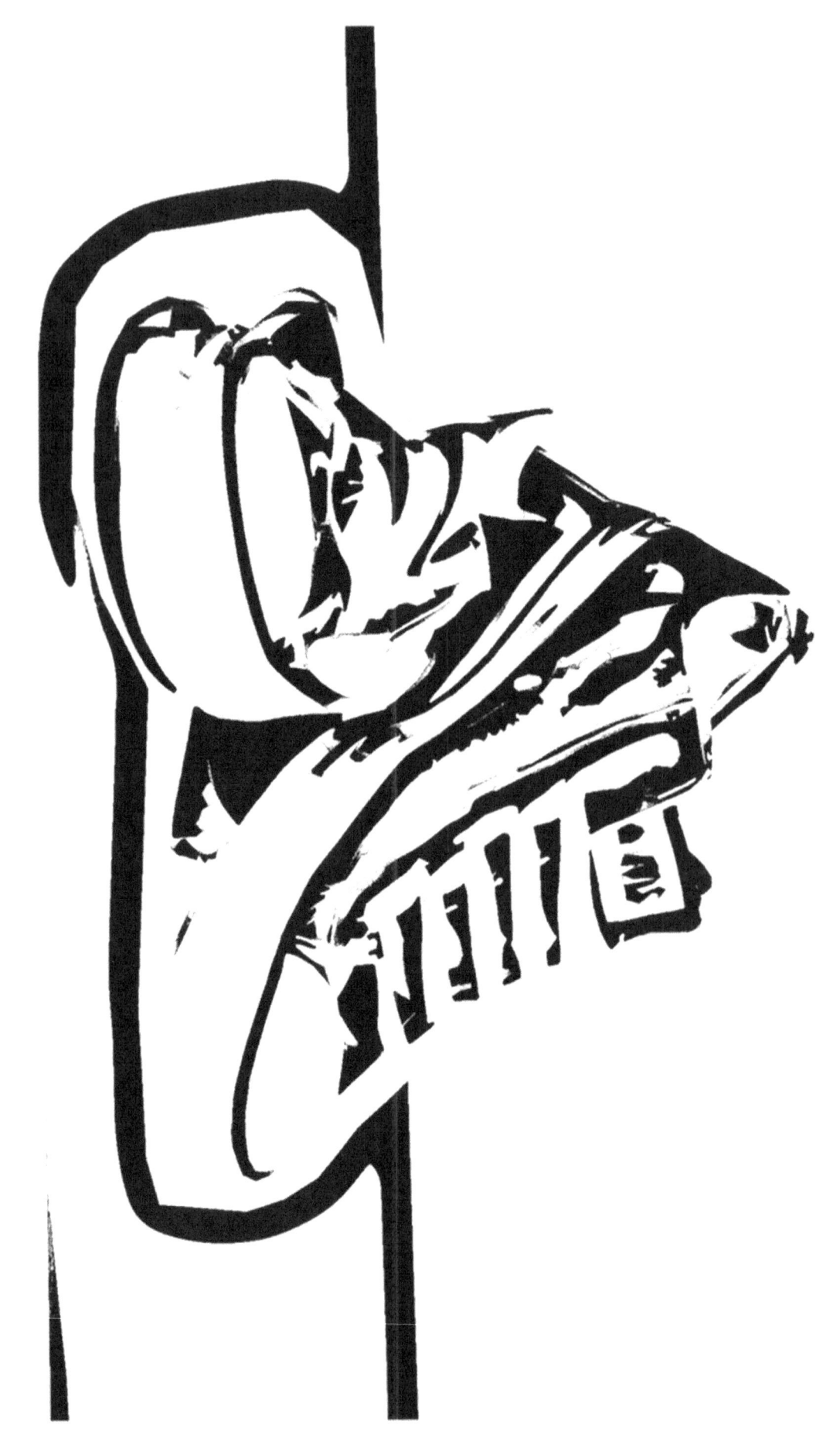

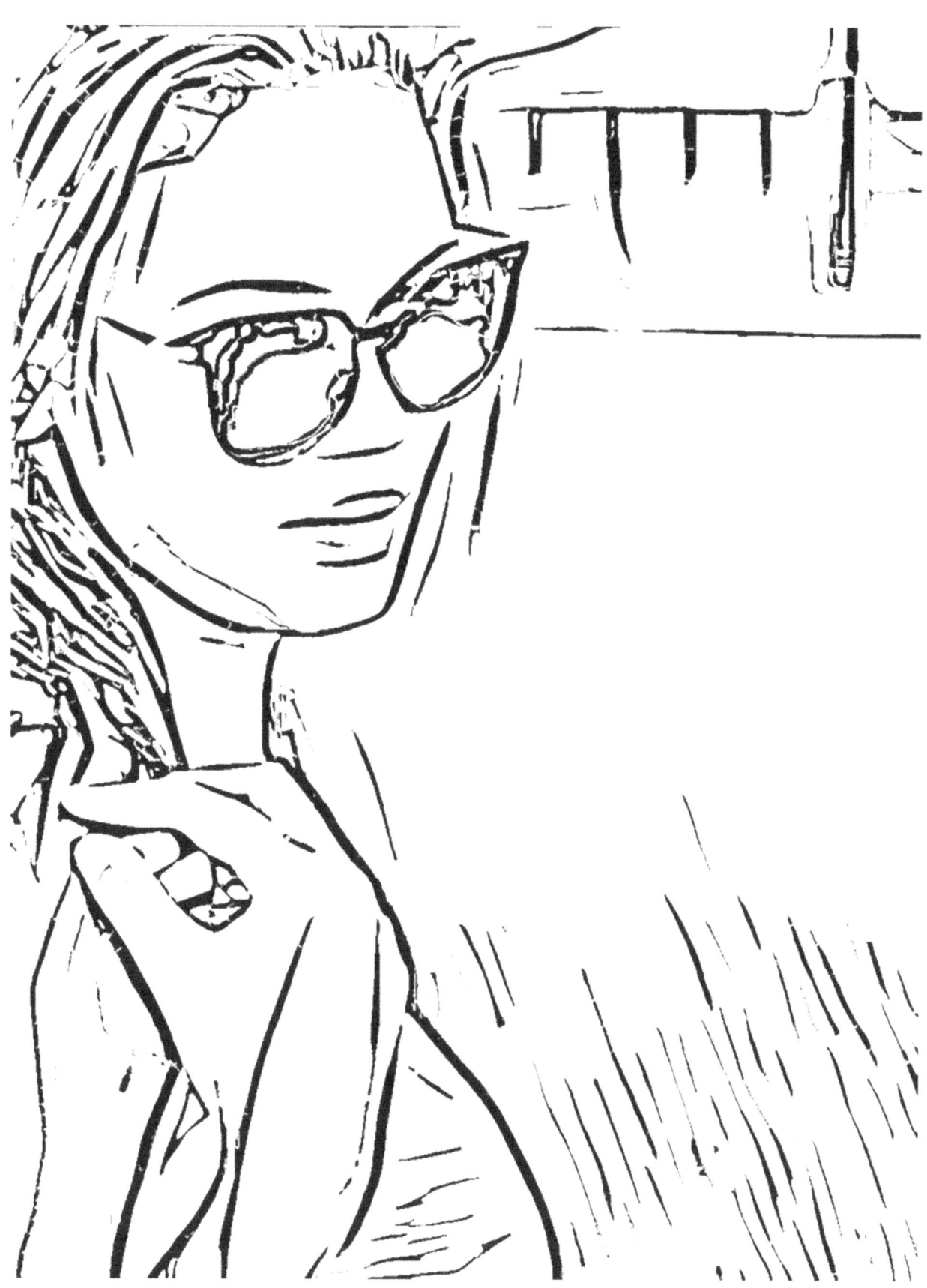

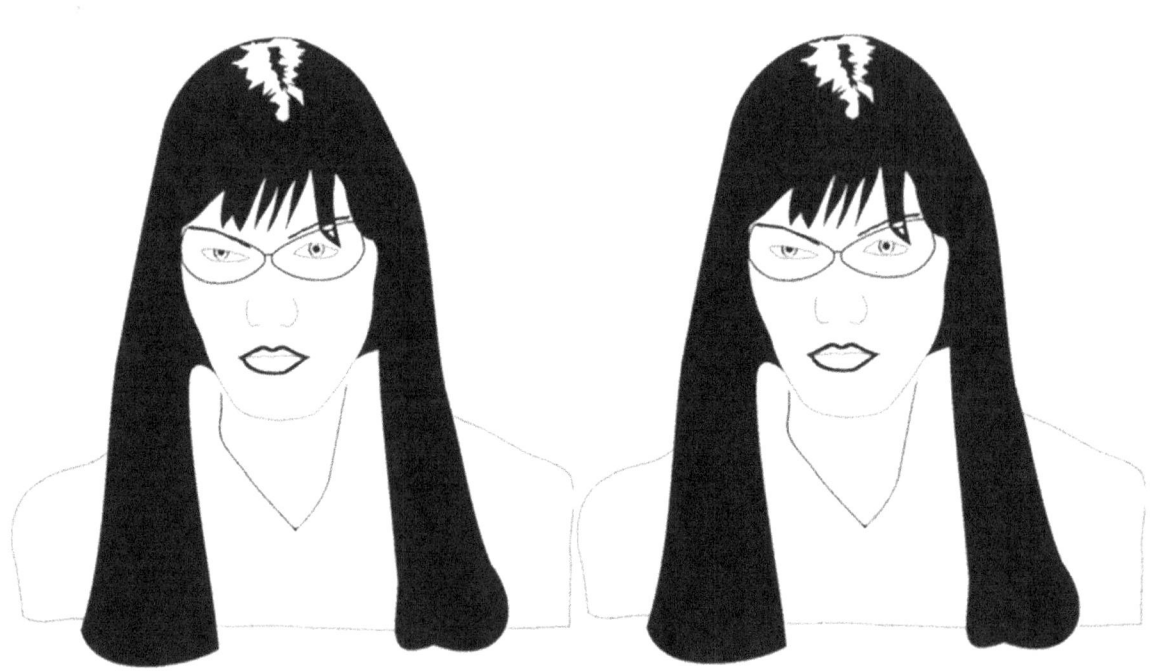

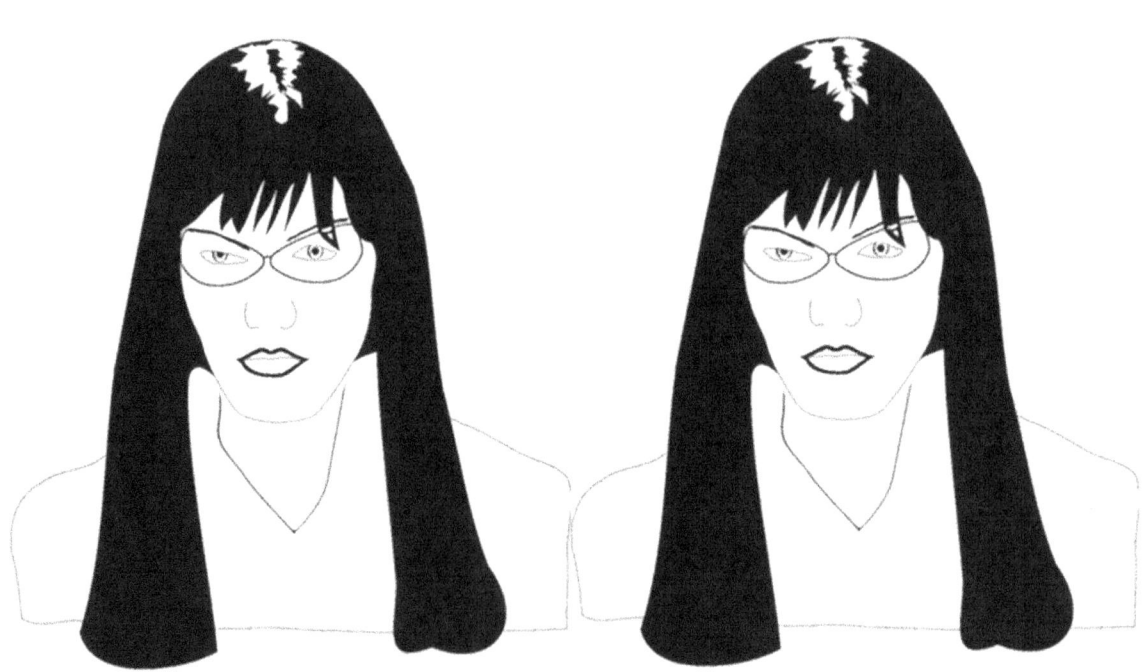

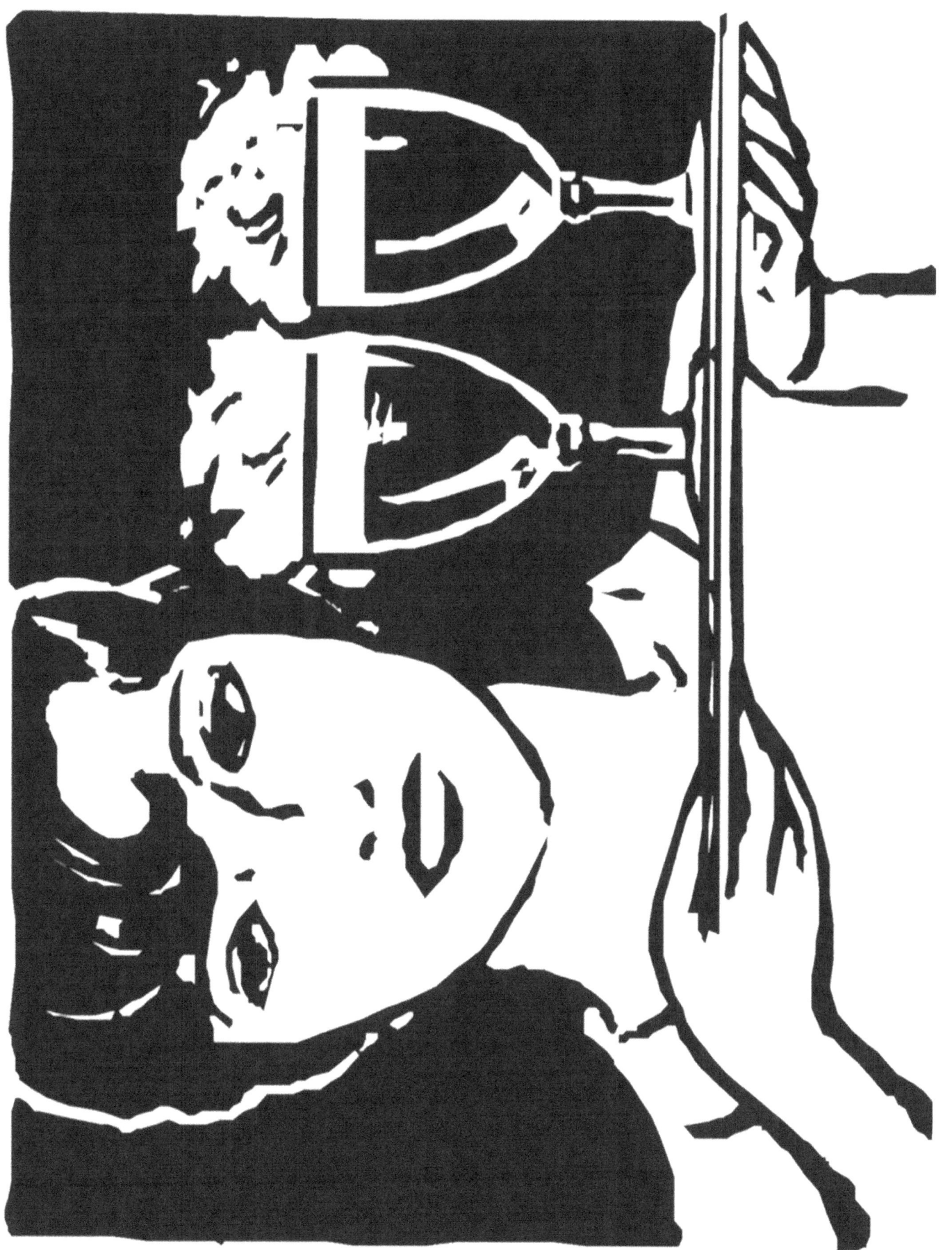

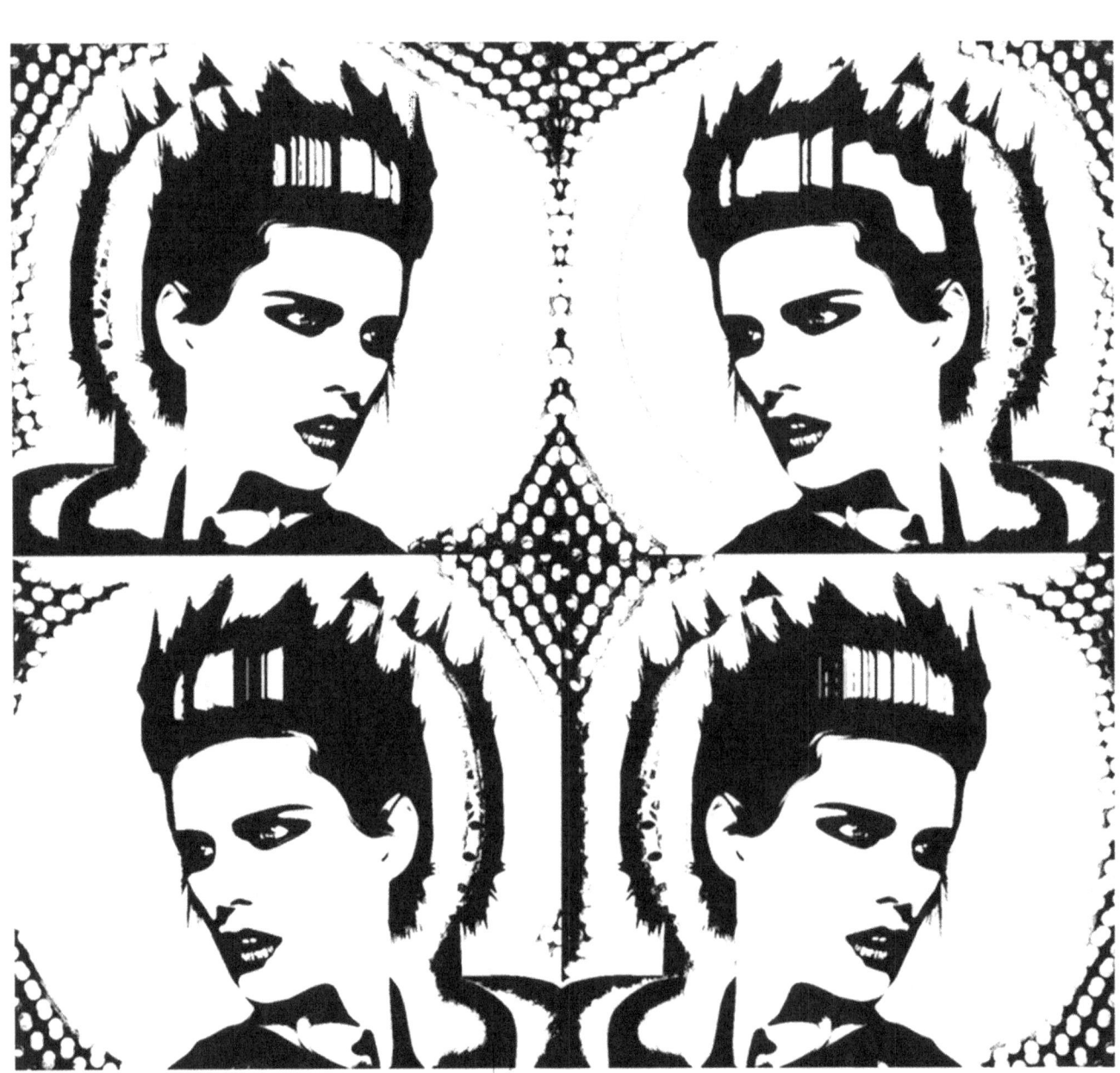

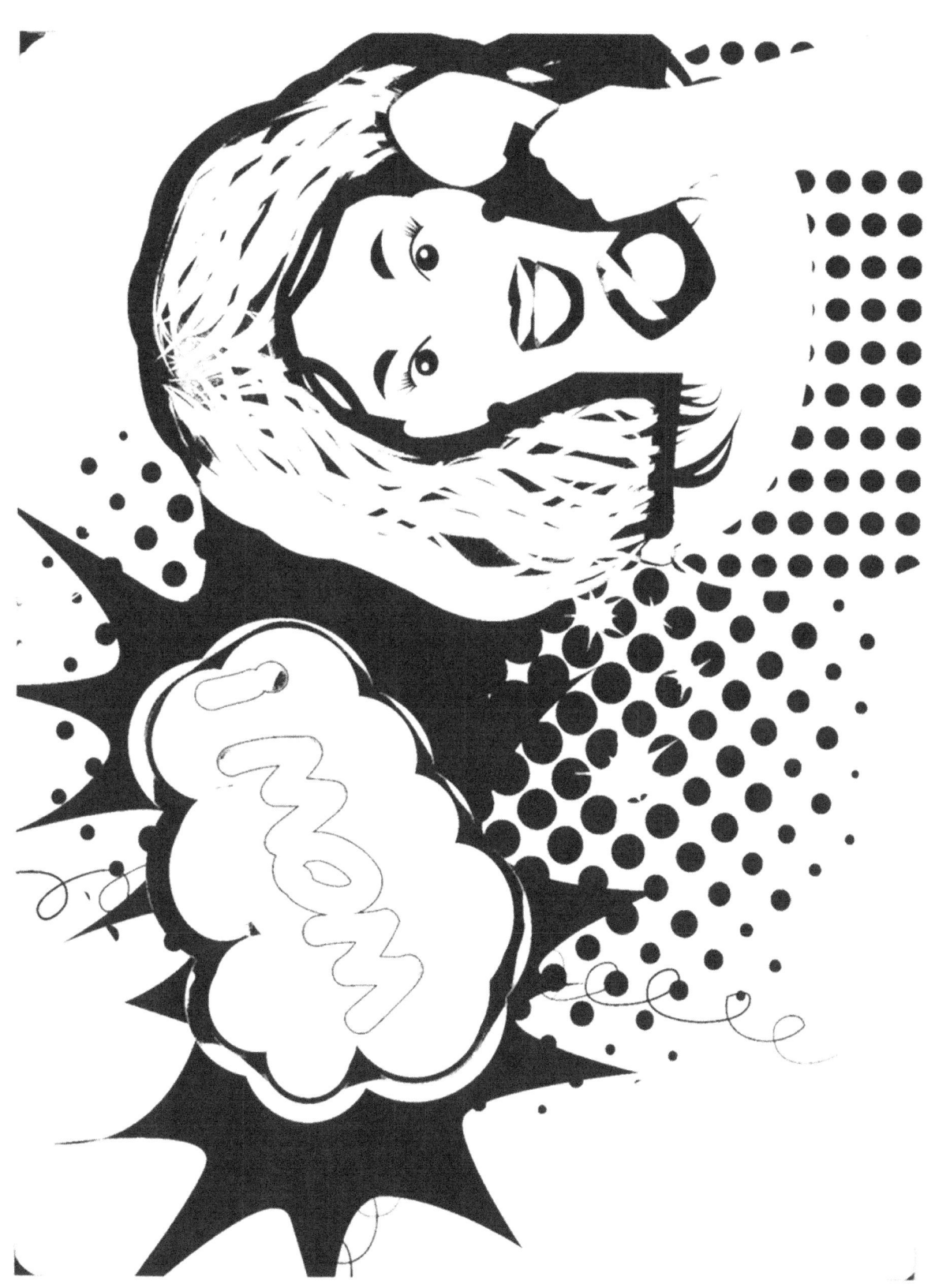

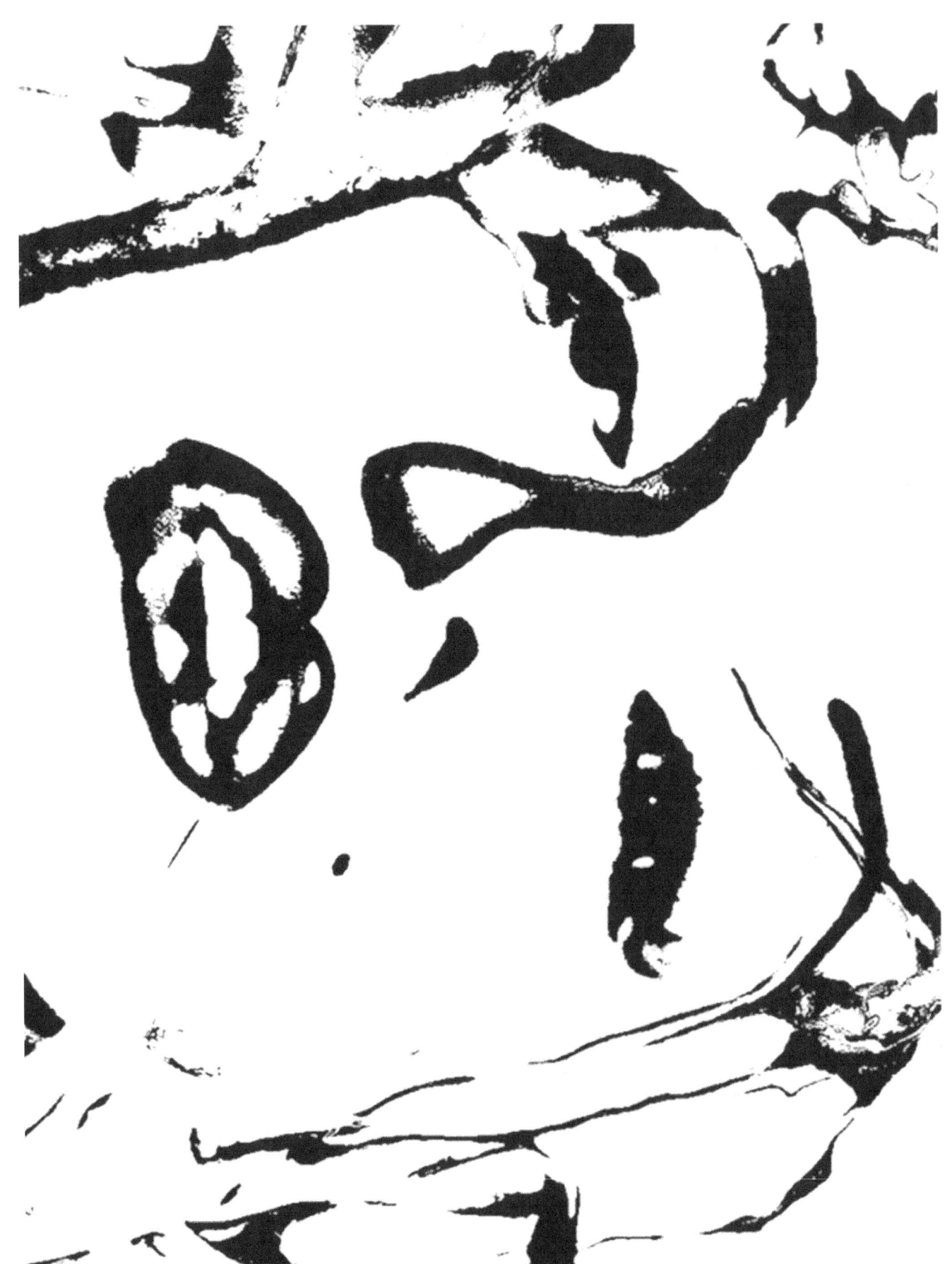

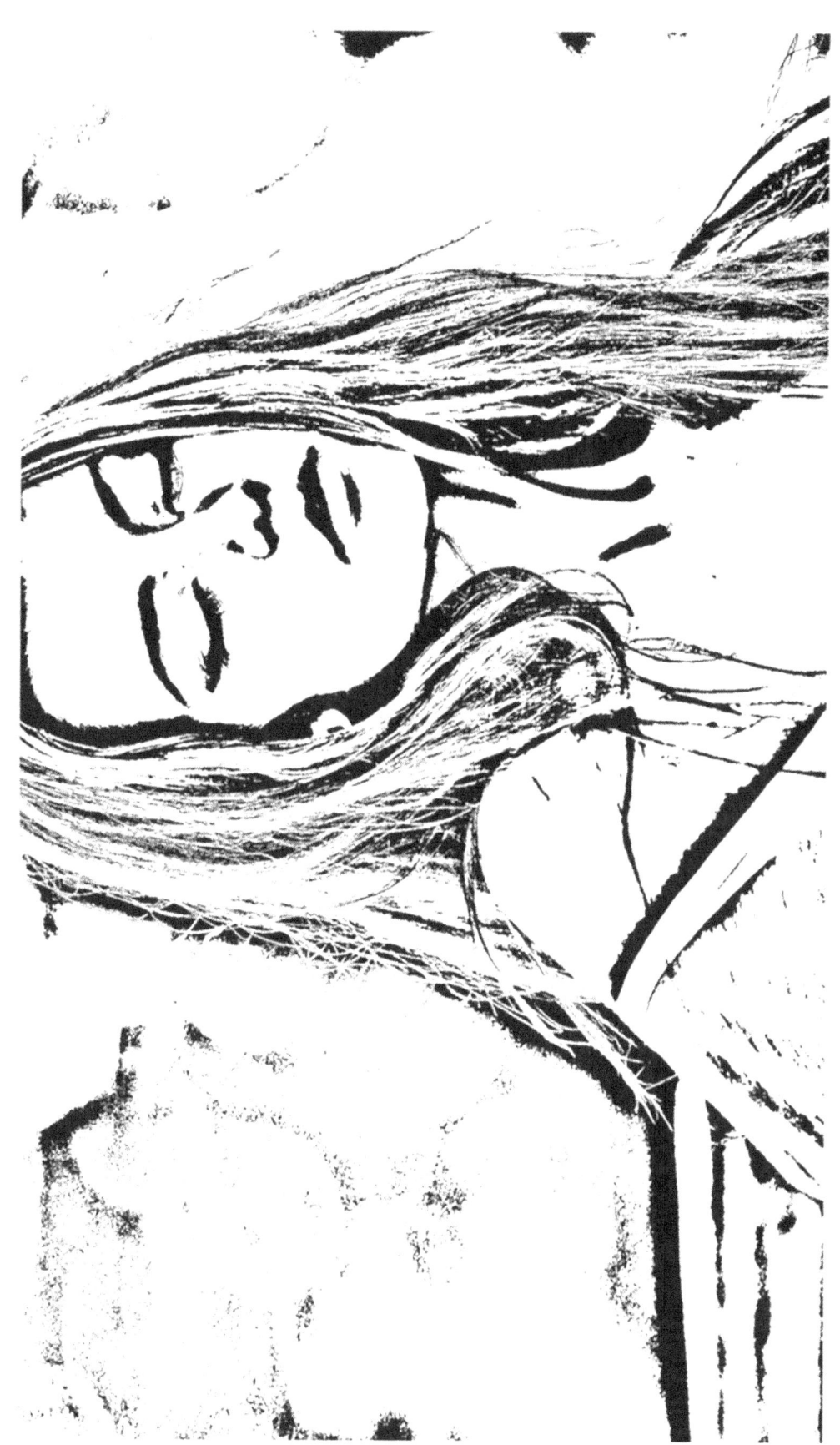

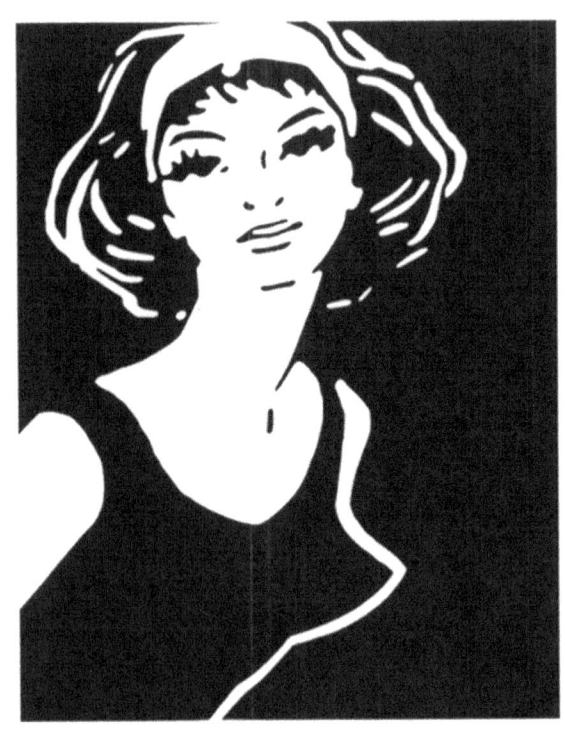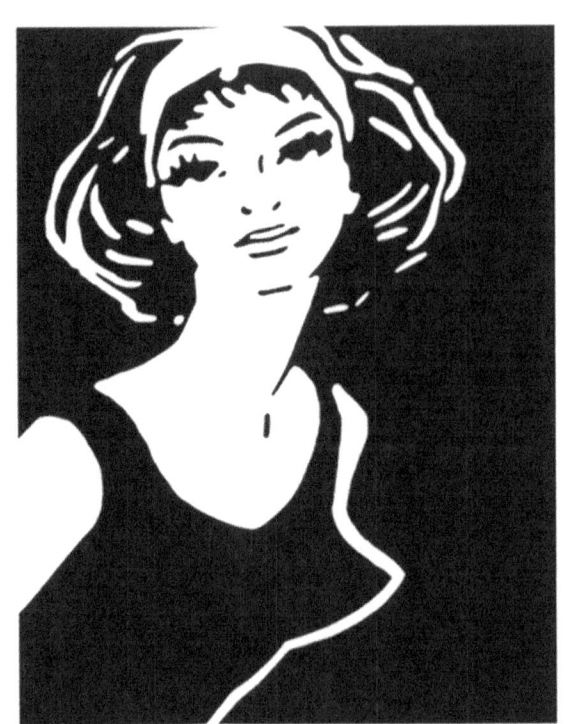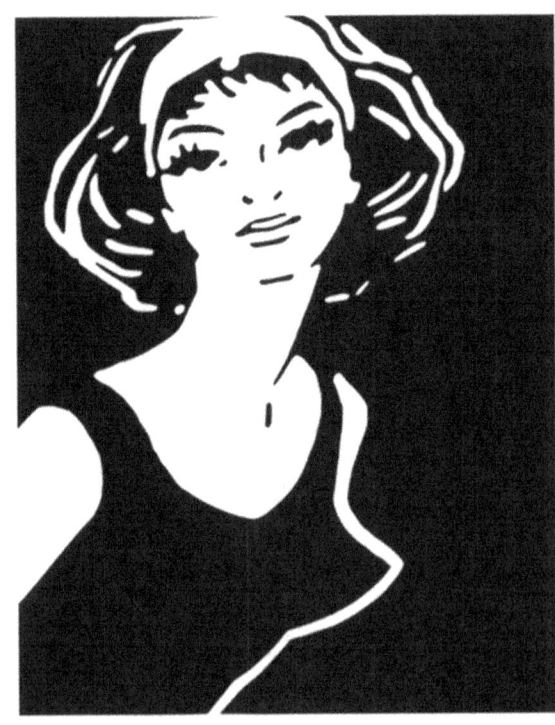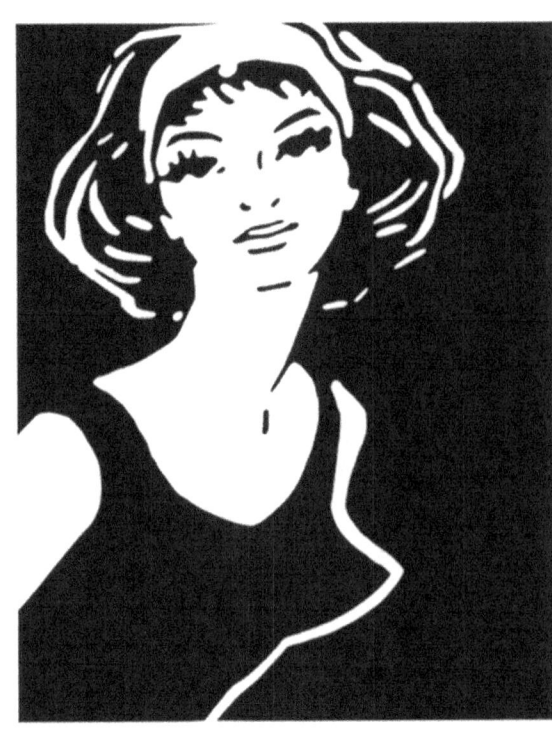

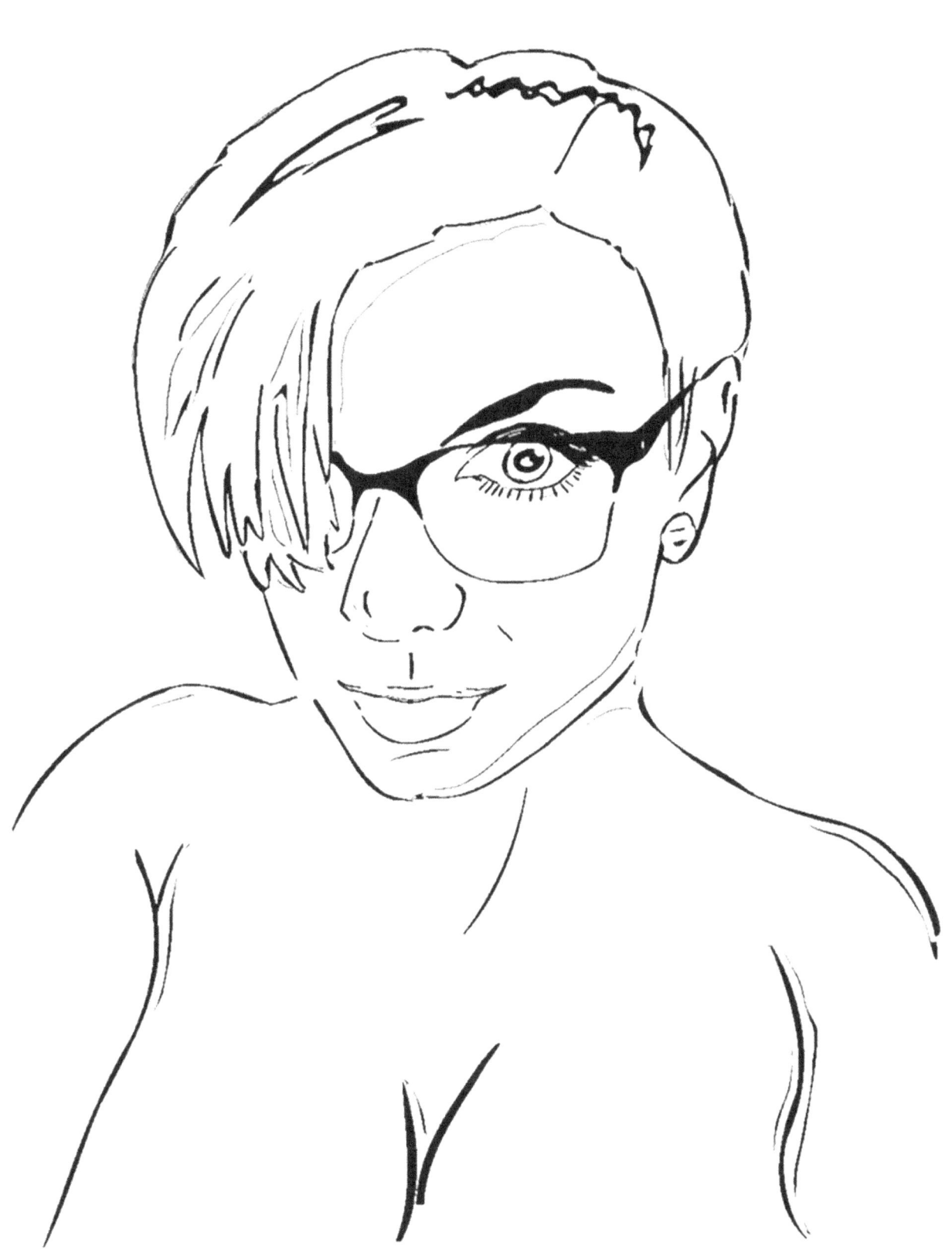

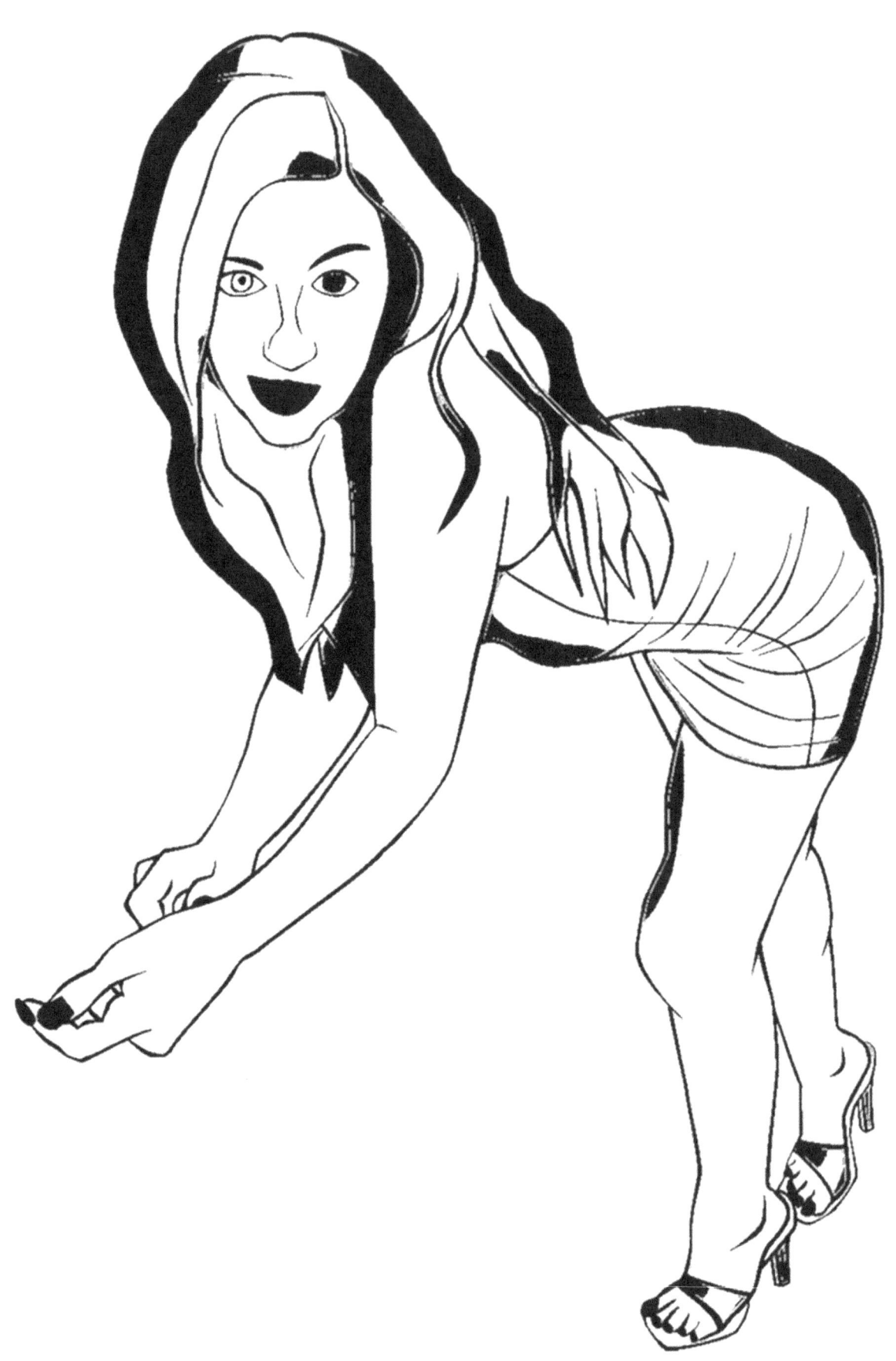

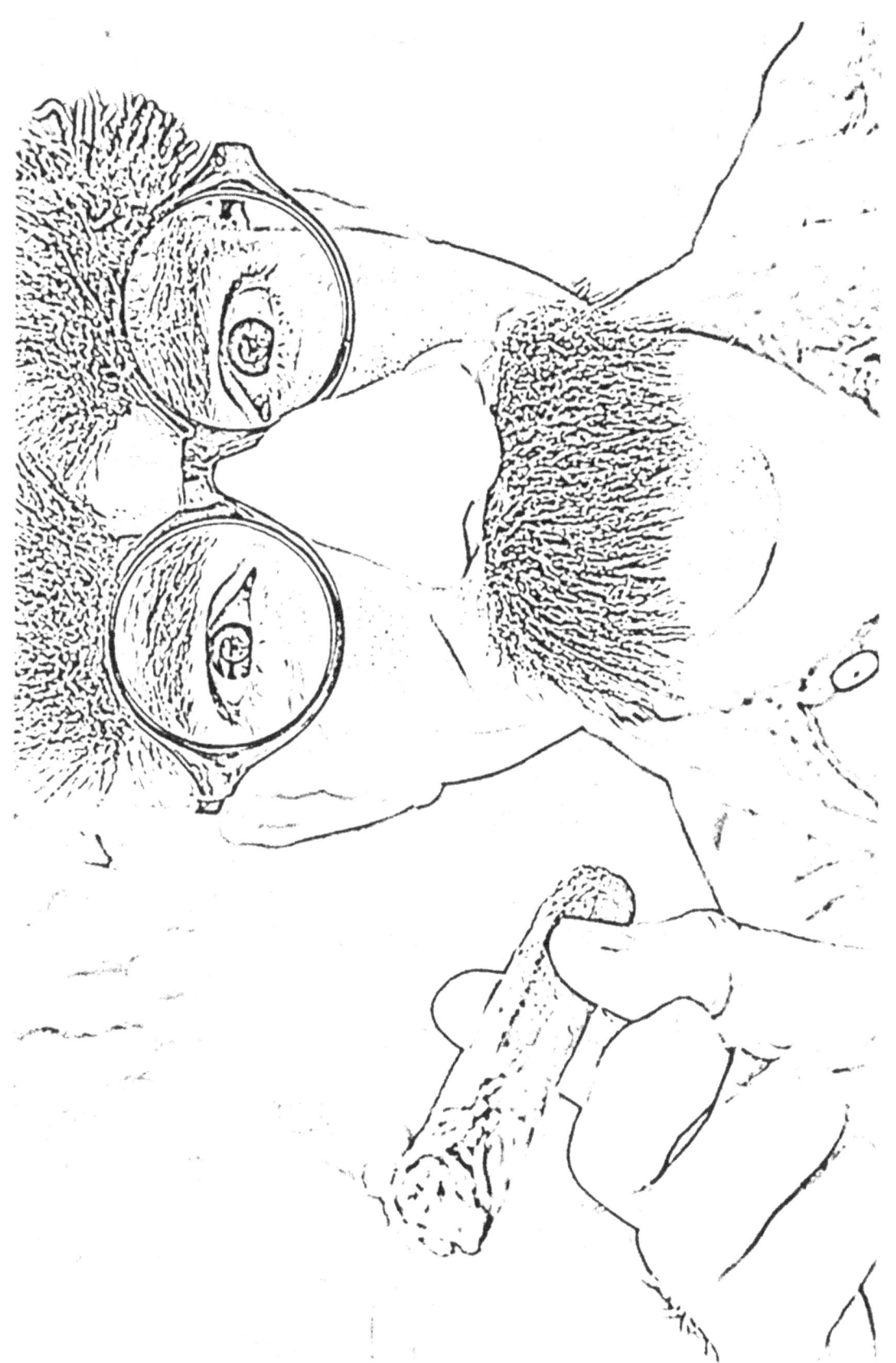

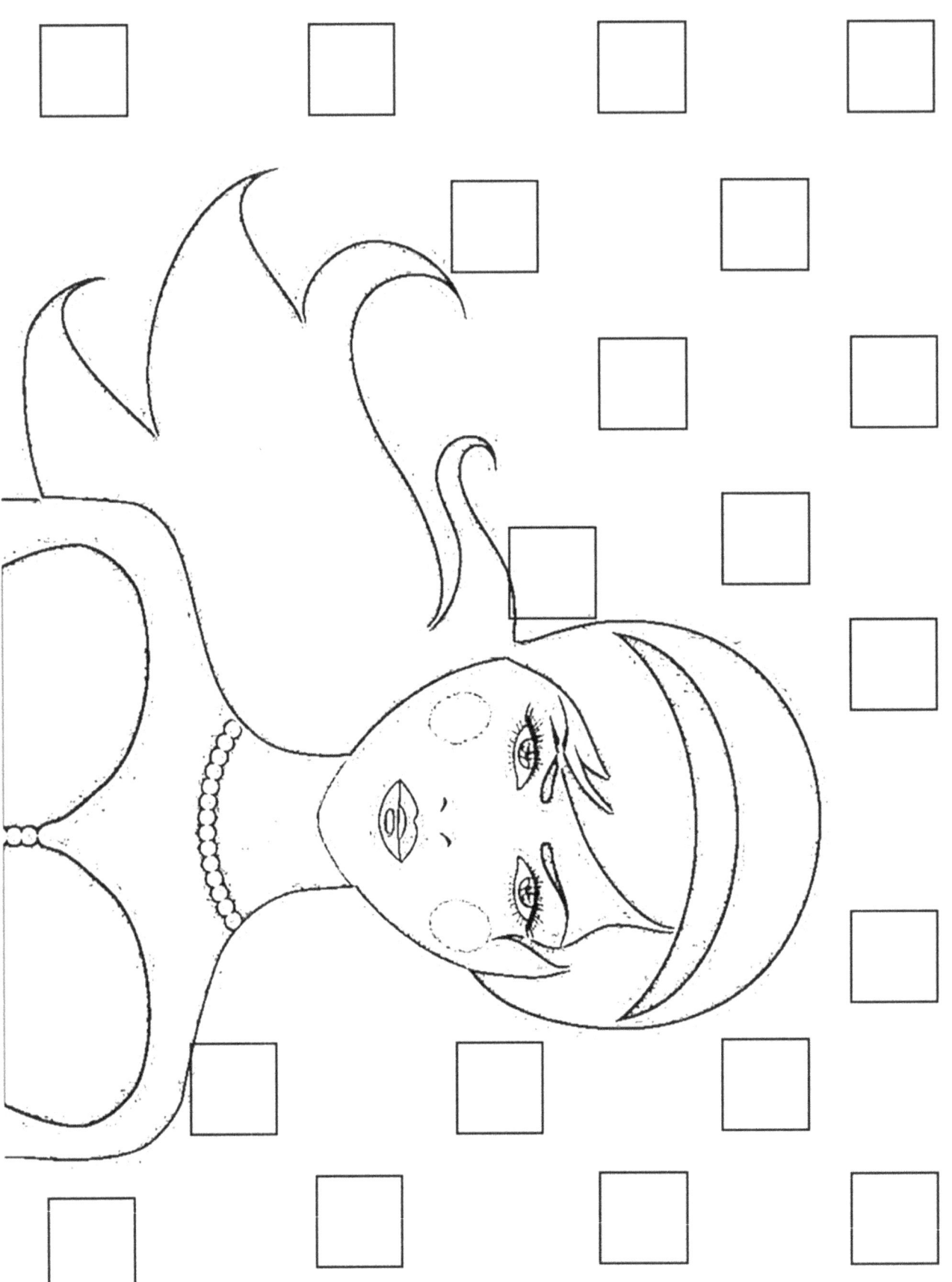

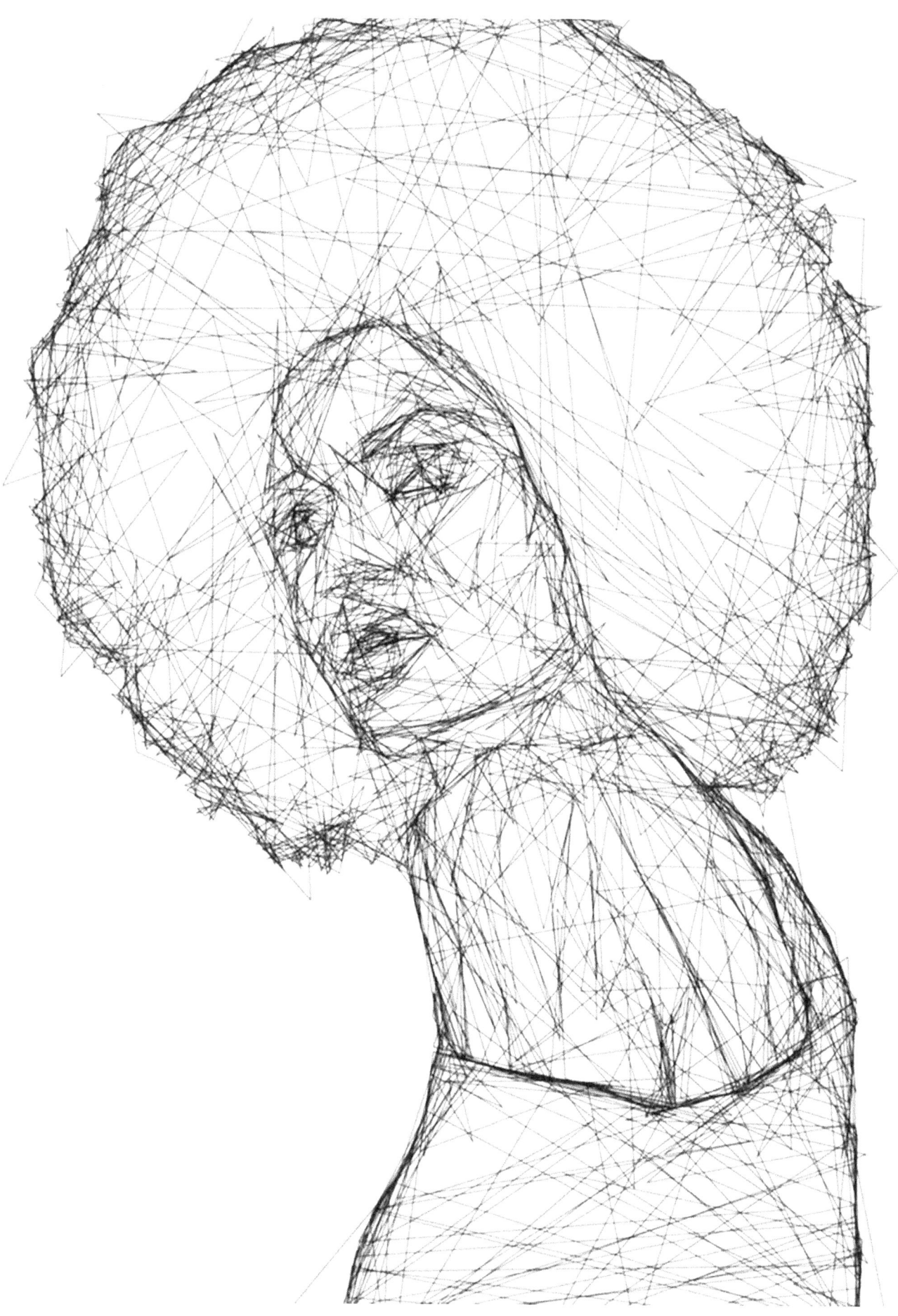

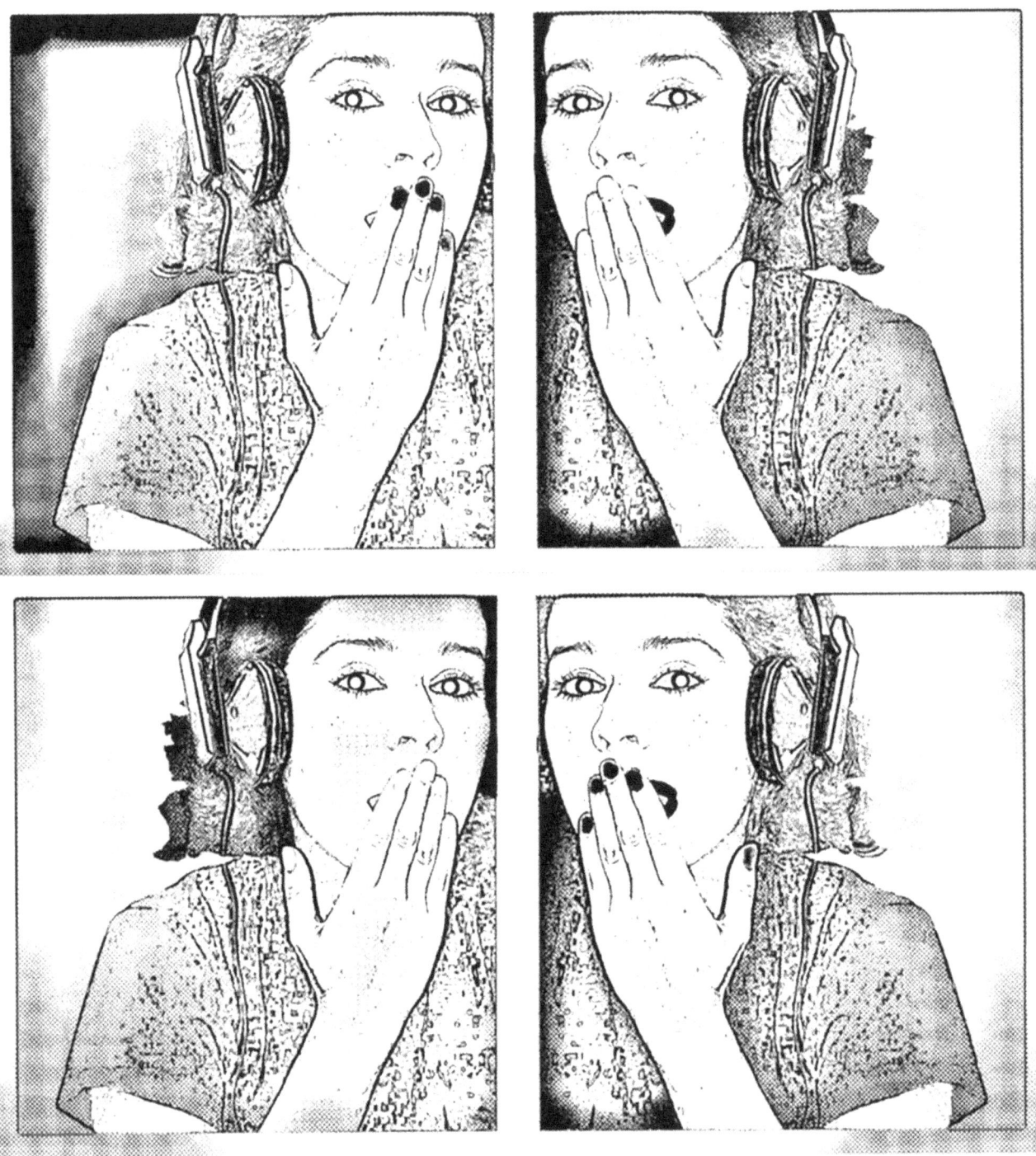

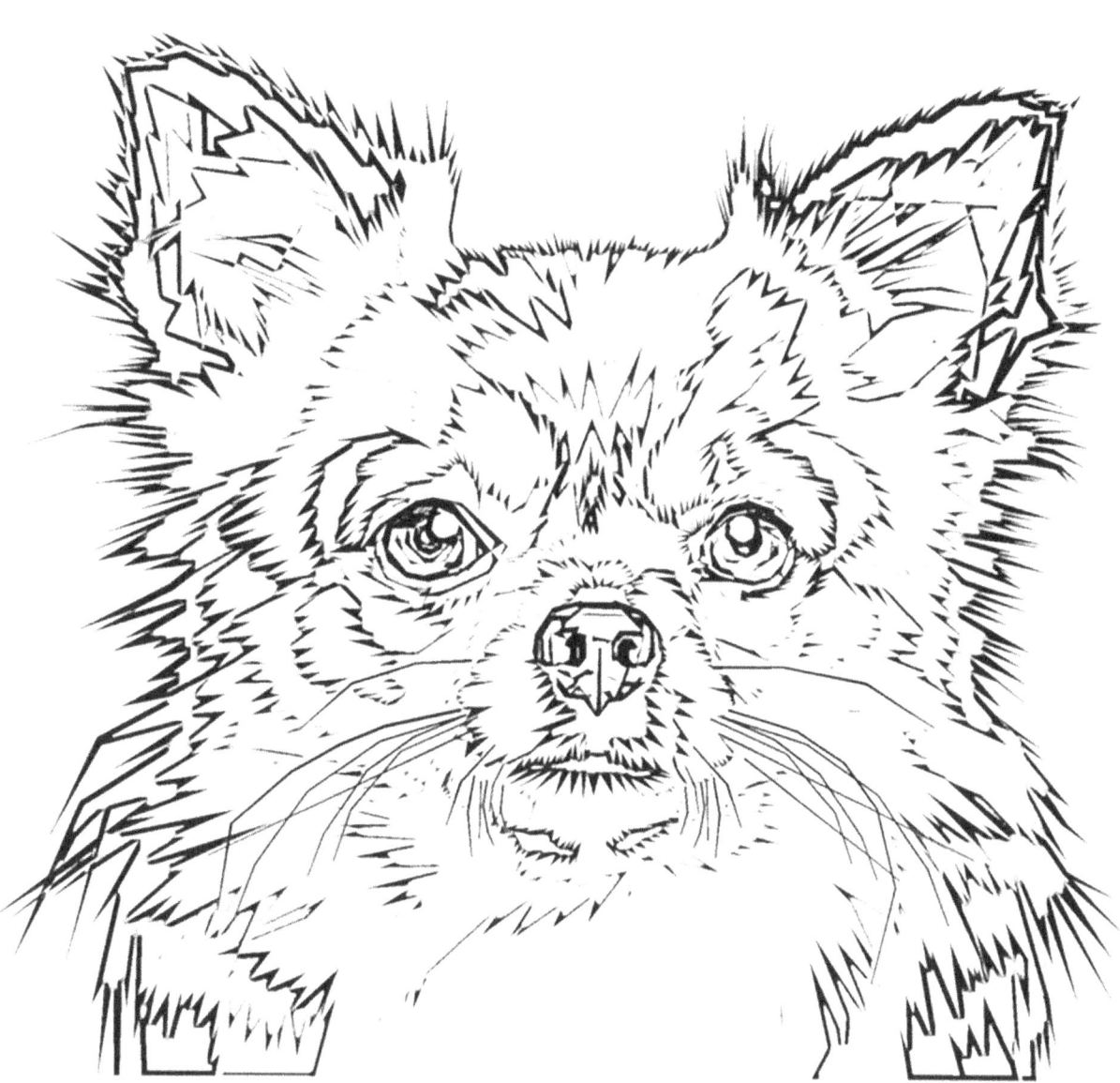

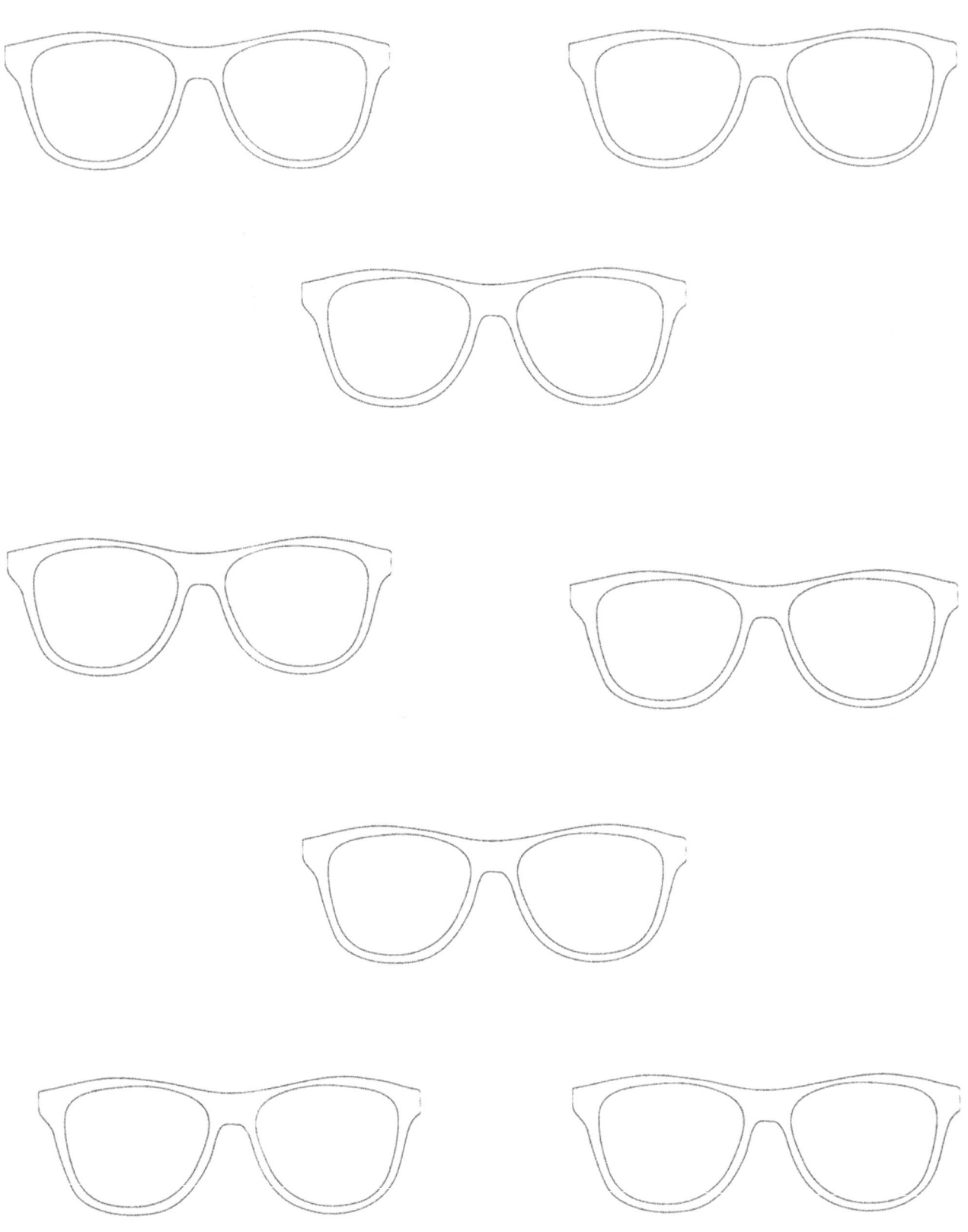

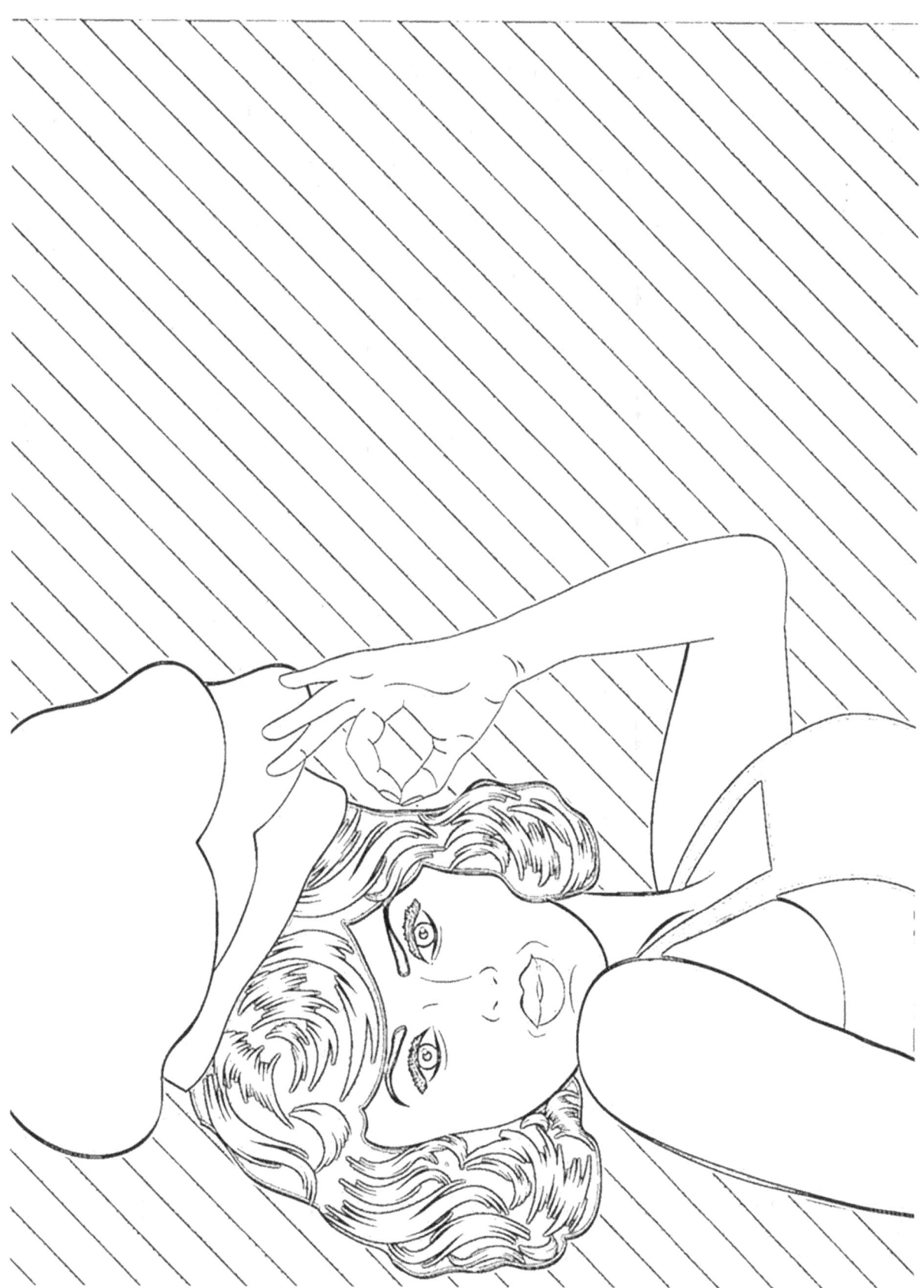

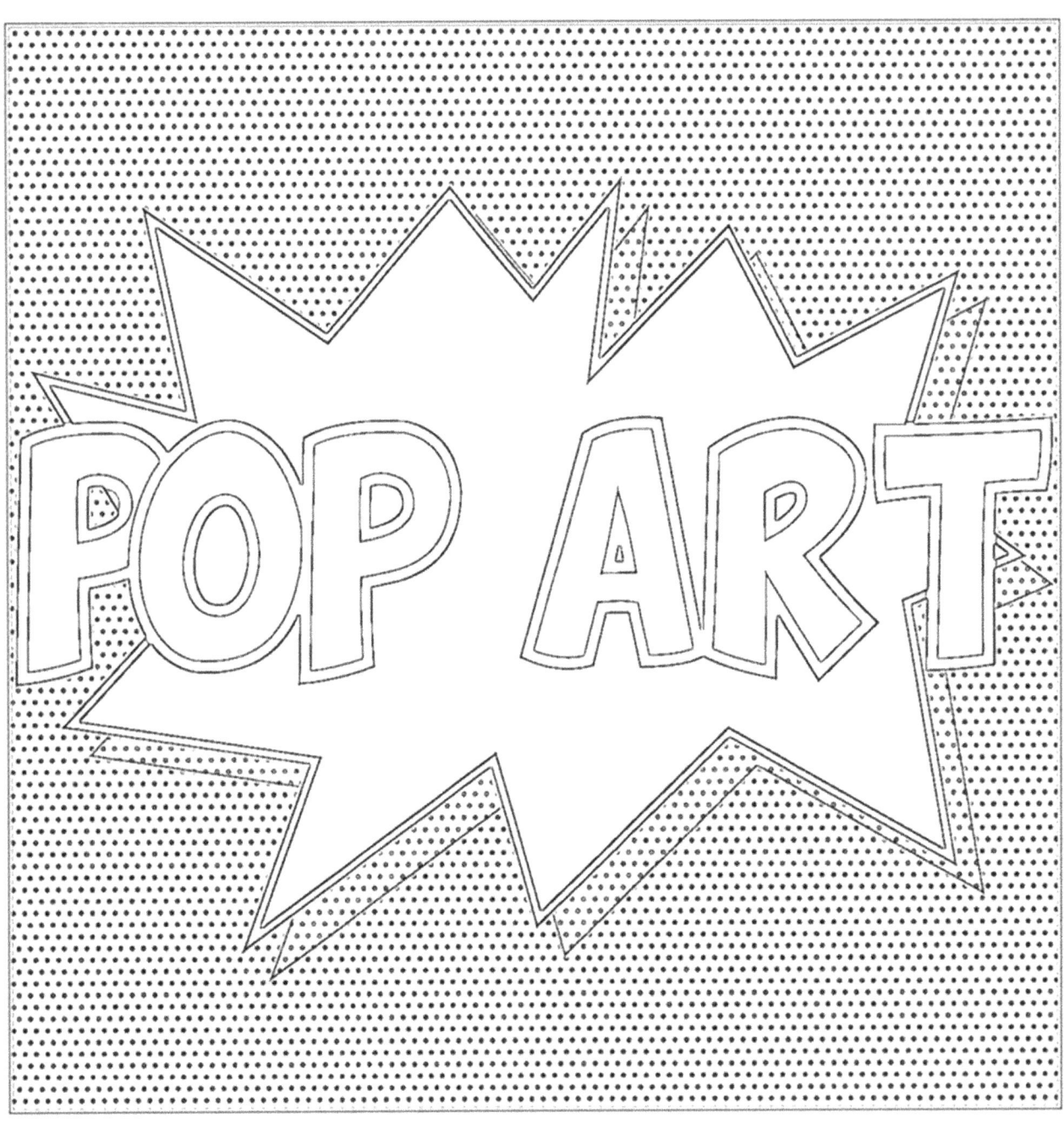

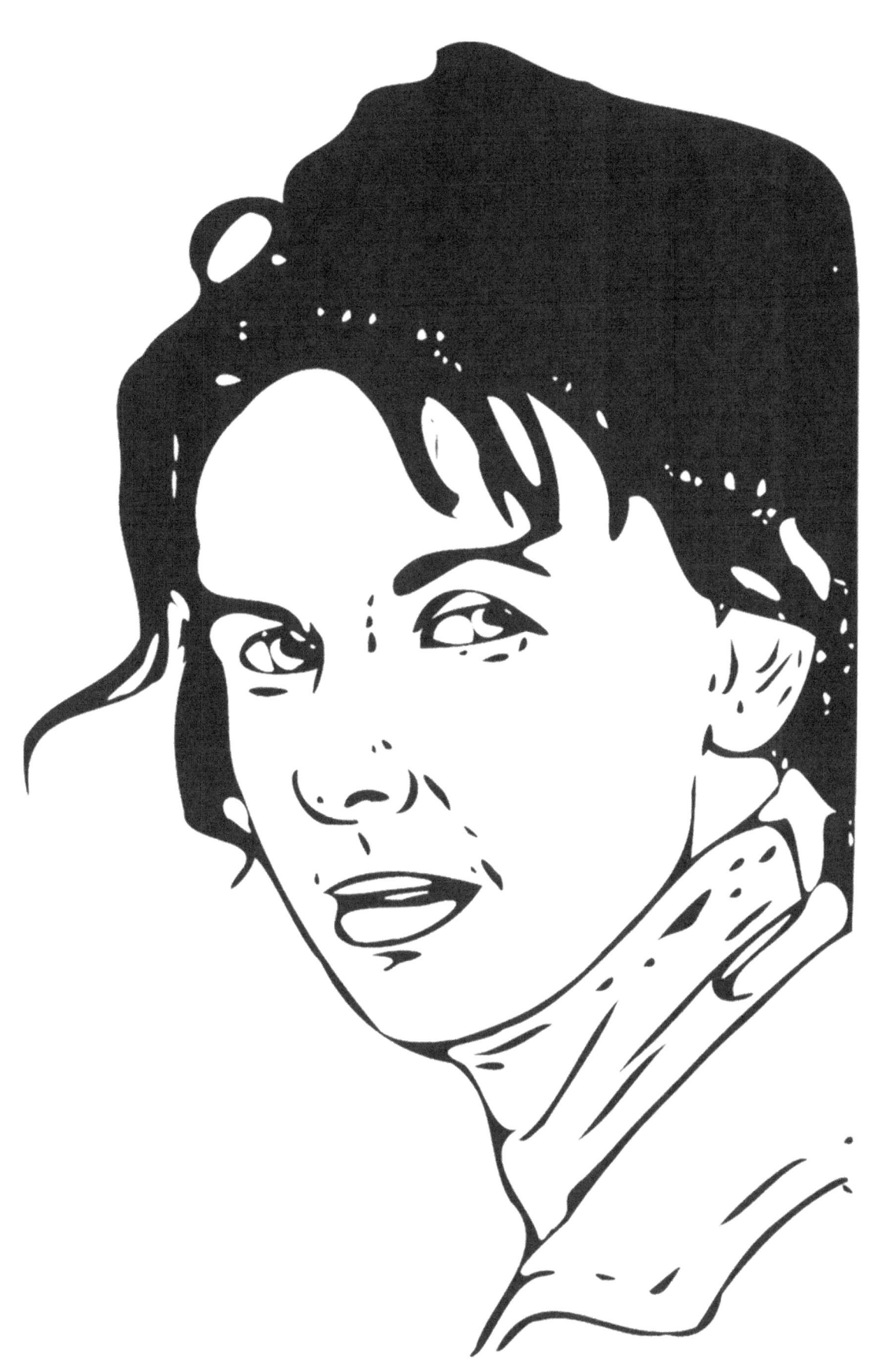

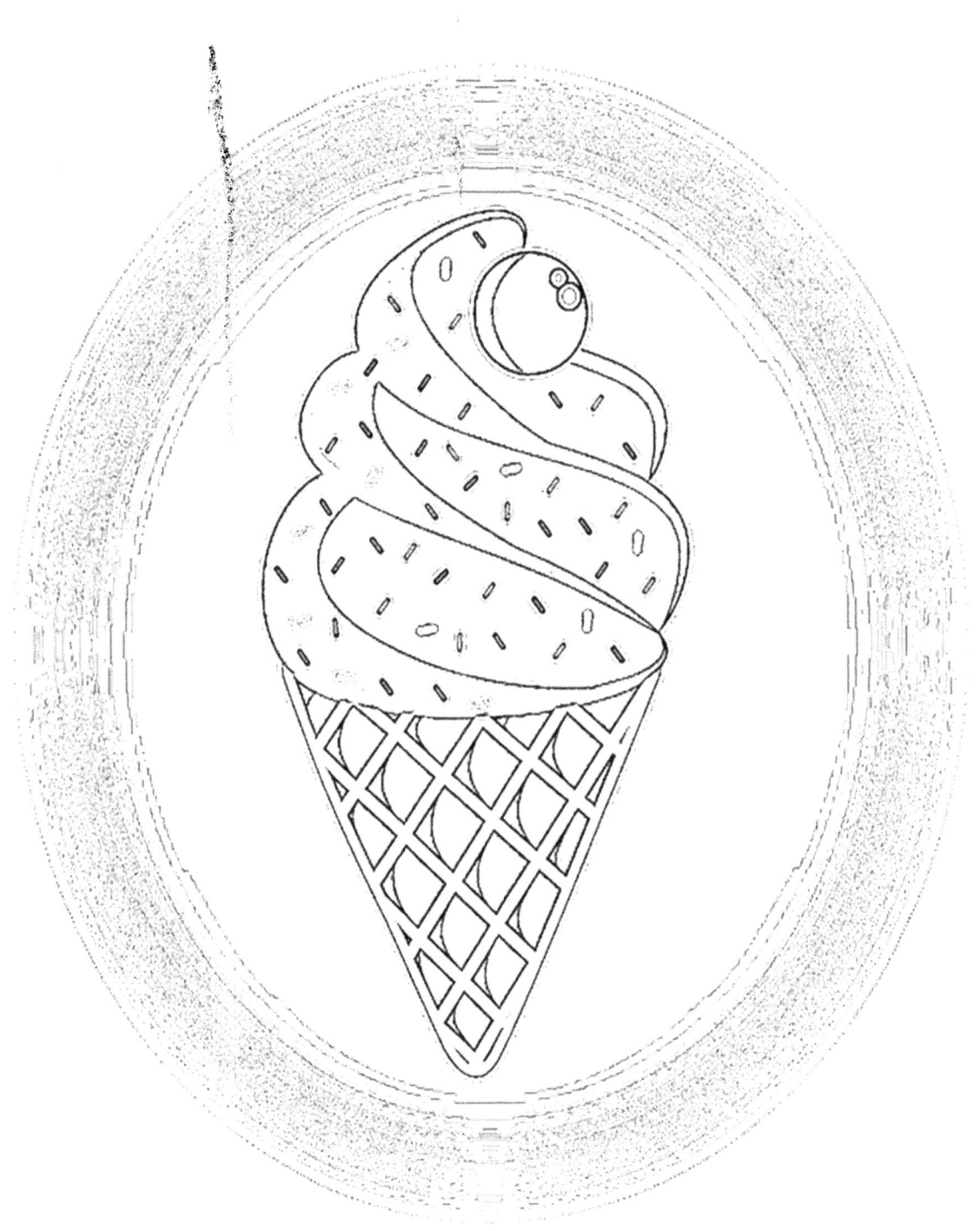

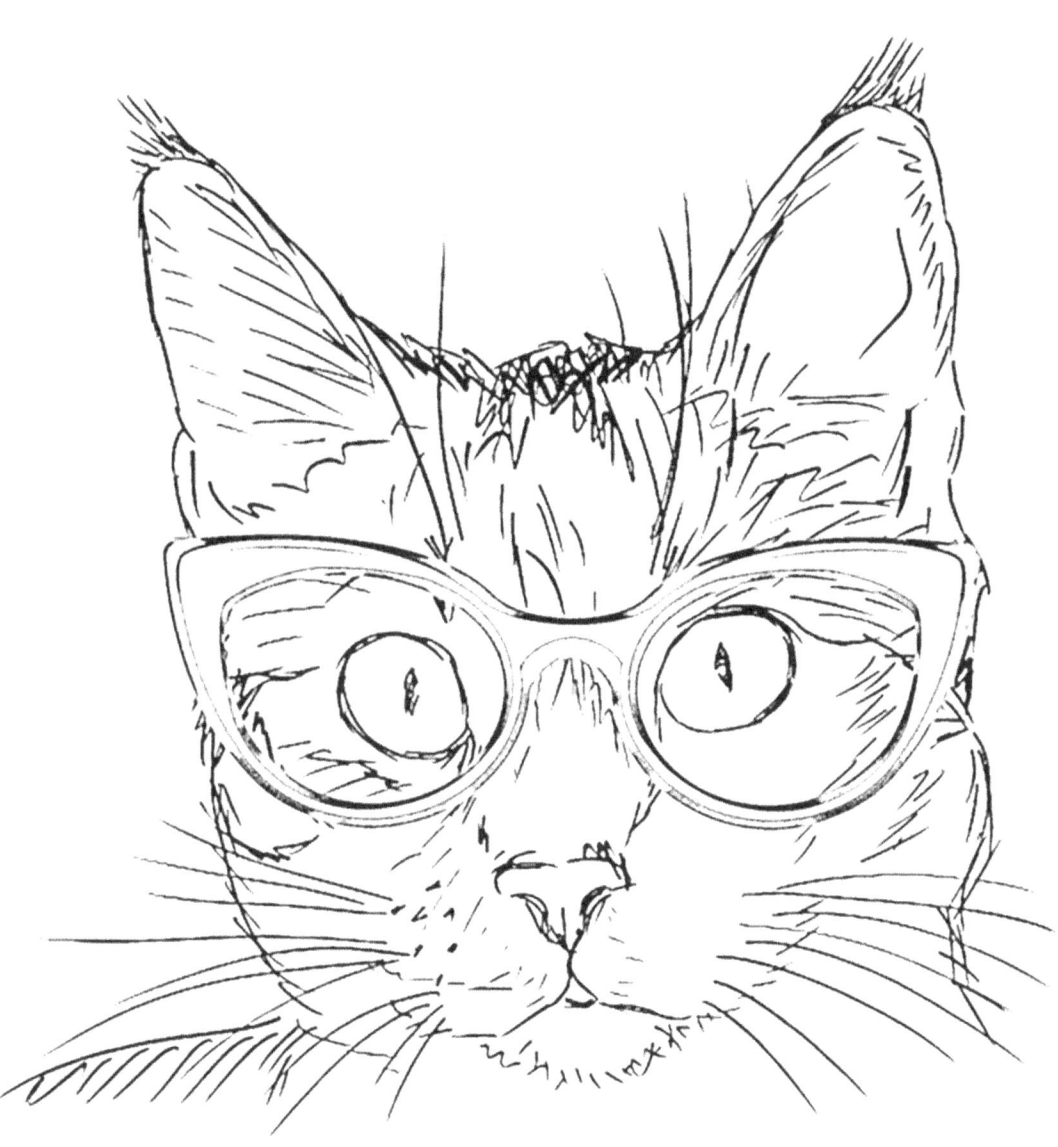

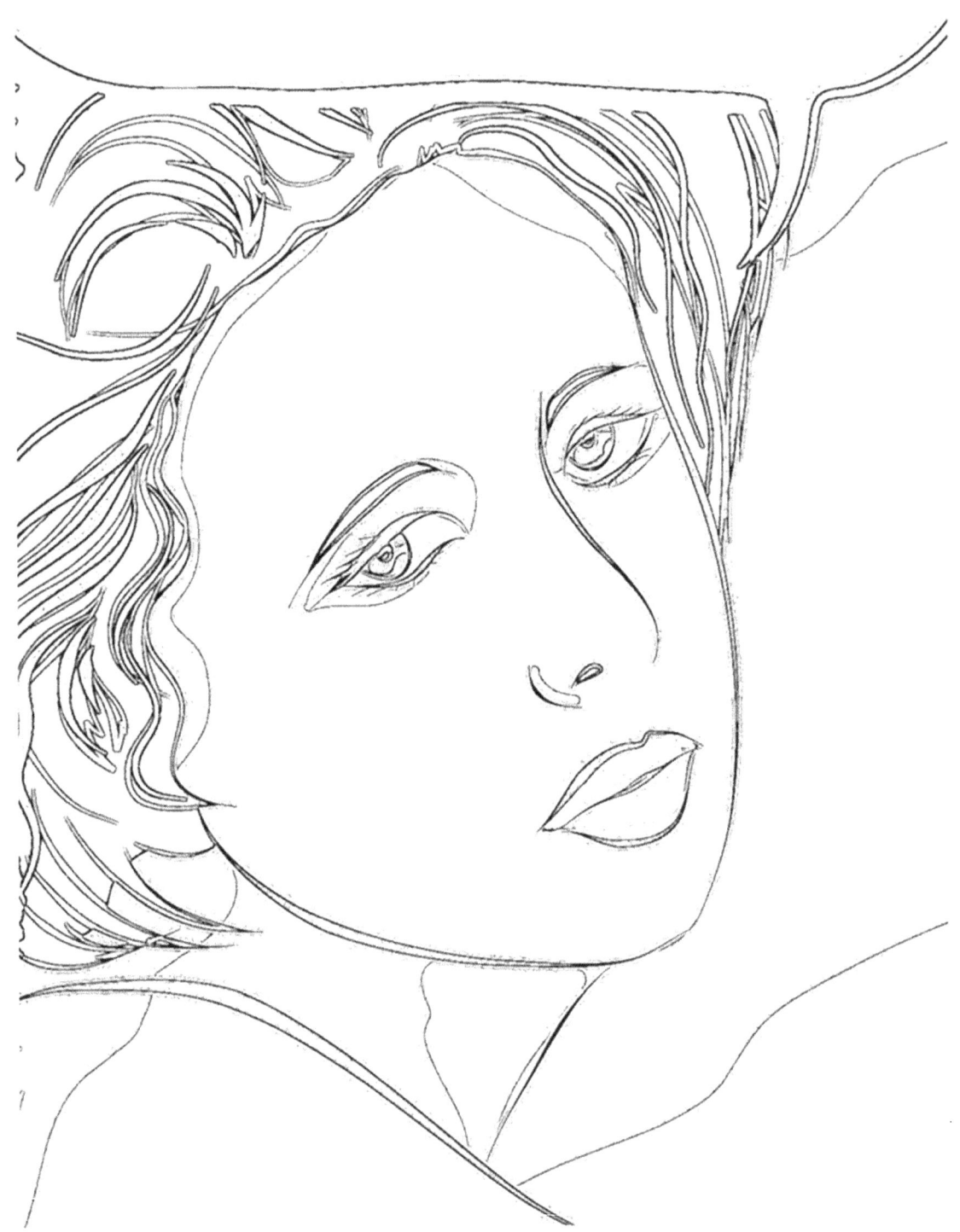

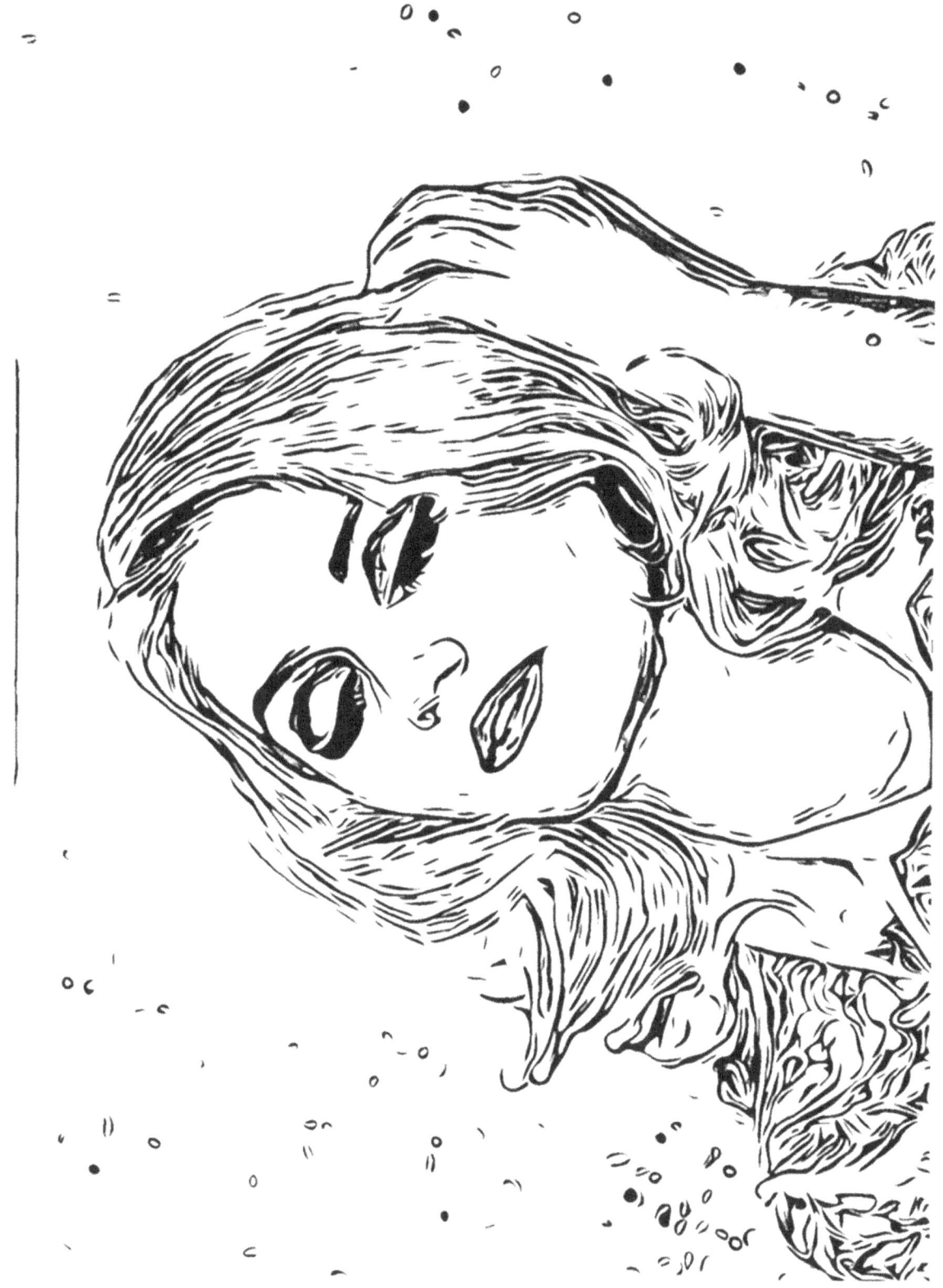

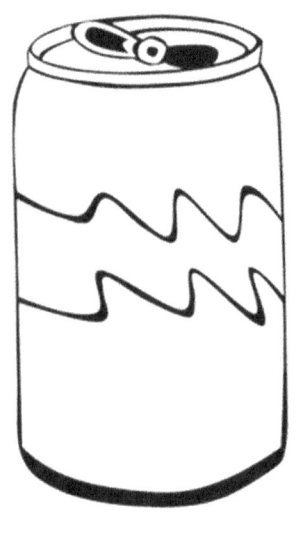
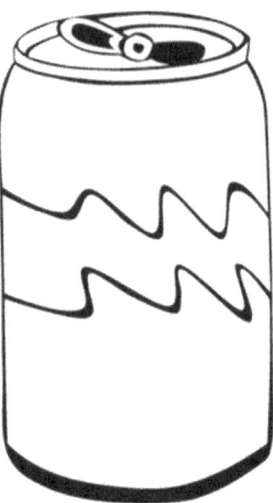
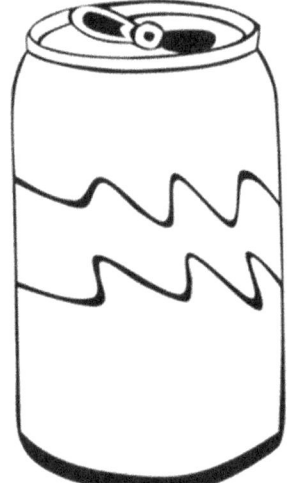
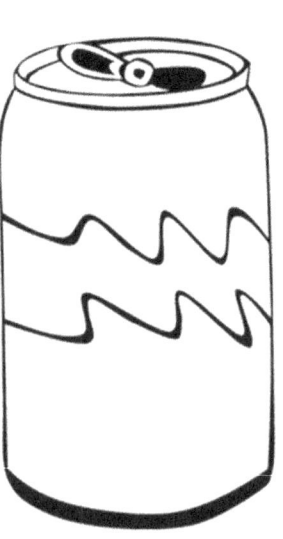

www.ingramcontent.com/pod-product-compliance
Lightning Source LLC
Chambersburg PA
CBHW081735220526
45468CB00008B/2114